CEREDIGION SHIPWRECKS

Tales of great courage and shameful behaviour

By
W Troughton

Published by:
Ystwyth Press
Swn-Y-Nant,
Cliff Terrace,
Aberystwyth,
Ceredigion,
SY23 2DN

ISBN0-9552125-0-2

Cover Picture
Shipwreck, presumably Cardigan Bay by Alfred Worthington, ca. 1900.
(Courtesy Amgueddfa Ceredigion)

Designed & Printed by Cambrian Printers, Aberystwyth.

List of Illustrations

Introduction

For those who don't know the area Ceredigion has sixty miles of beautiful coastline, much of it rugged and rocky but also blessed with stretches of golden sand. This beauty was little appreciated by mariners in the days of sail. Most were happy to give this spectacular shore a wide berth unless their business took them to one of the settlements nestled between the cliffs. Ceredigion being a lee shore with no natural harbour it is inevitable that even experienced mariners stood the chance of being caught out by the vagaries of wind and tide. Keeping far out to sea lessened the chances of becoming acquainted with this inhospitable coast. If the physical environment seemed hostile then this was nothing compared to the treatment shipwrecked sailors could expect if they found themselves ashore. Writing in 1743 Howell Harris, the religious reformer, condemned the people of New Quay for their inhuman behaviour towards shipwrecked mariners who, he asserted, 'would rather fall among the heathen' than into the hands of those living on the Cardiganshire coast. At least one Portuguese sailor coming ashore at Borth would concur (see Chapter 5).

It was precious little comfort for these unfortunates to know that they were in exalted company - the first recorded shipwreck on the coast of Ceredigion was no less than Saint Ina, wrecked near New Quay. In gratitude for his safe deliverance he founded the church at Llanina. The shameful behaviour of looting wrecked ships continued until the mid nineteenth century and has often masked the great courage of many men who risked (and sometimes gave) their lives to help total strangers.

There must also have been many other casualties over the centuries. It is difficult to imagine that the maritime trade associated with Strata Florida Abbey and the castles at Cardigan and Aberystwyth did not lead to casualties locally. From the eighteenth century onwards there is a steady flow of brief accounts recounting the loss of lives and property along the Ceredigion coast. This book includes some 170 of these, varying from modest fishing smacks to a 7,000 ton ocean liner. Most date from the eighteenth and nineteenth centuries when shipping was at it's zenith and before the plethora of electronic aids available to today's mariners were invented. Despite the changes in transport that have seen railways and roads replace shipping one thing that has remained unchanged is the sixty miles of beautiful coastline. Where possible I have attempted to list the nature of each vessel wrecked such as tonnage, rig, when and where built etc. The paucity of this information for many of the earlier wrecks is reflected in the text.

A Note on Sources

To the aspiring researcher the most useful source of information on shipwrecks are newspapers. The earliest paper to carry details of shipwrecks was Lloyds List, which started publication (and a constant battle to understand Welsh place-names) in 1741. In the early nineteenth century news pertaining to Cardiganshire was to be found in the Swansea-published *Cambrian.* Later both the *Carmarthen Journal* and the *Carnarvon & Denbigh* Herald (1831) took sufficient interest in the affairs of the county to report maritime activities. Cardiganshire had no local newspapers until the publication of the *Cardigan & Tivyside Advertiser* in 1855 and the *Aberystwyth Observer* in 1858. Both these papers owed their existence to the repeal of stamp duty on newspapers in 1855. Prior to this newspapers were an expensive luxury even for those who could read. The repeal of stamp duty and the opportunities for distribution offered by the railway network saw newspapers become far more popular. Many local newspapers at this time came partly pre-printed from London with national advertisements, political and international news provided, along with juicy murders or other sensational crimes of the day. Blank spaces were left for the local newspaper offices to put in their more parochial news, editorials and advertisements.

Other than newspapers there are many diverse sources that can provide information on maritime disasters. Shipping registers sometimes contain at the very least clues to a vessel's demise, often in a terse line 'Vessel lost off Cardigan Head, 3 lives lost (*Morning Star*, 1859) or 'totally lost near Aberystwyth 8th Sept' (*Theodosia,* 1831). Fortunately registers for both Aberystwyth and Cardigan registered vessels are very useful in this respect. Both seem to have been kept up to date with pride. Registers for larger ports tend to contain less detail, perhaps because of the relative anonymity of the vessels and masters. In smaller ports such as Aberystwyth and Cardigan the owners and masters of these vessels were known personally to those responsible for maintaining the registers. Crew agreements detailing wages, provisions and the nature of the voyage to be expected were first introduced in 1863. As many of the vessels that came to grief on the coast of Ceredigion were local these agreements often contain a brief note on the demise of their vessels. Far greater details are to be found in the depositions made by the captain and other crew to the local Receiver of Wreck under the Merchant Shipping Act 1854. These were given on oath as soon as possible after a vessel's demise and contain in great detail the sequence of events leading to a ships loss. Those collected by the Aberystwyth Receiver of Wreck can be consulted at the National Archives in Kew. These depositions frequently served as the basis for subsequent newspaper accounts of shipwrecks.

Another, older, source of information on local shipwrecks is the Cardigan Gaol Files, which along with details of numerous petty crimes and legal disputes include inquests. Occasionally these are into deaths resulting from shipwreck, either directly or in the case of Aberporth in 1816, indirectly. Sadly, those pertaining to luckless fishermen caught out by wind or tide appear regularly amongst these inquests.

Occasional mention of shipwrecks are to be found in the estate papers of the local gentry, either as a result of their legal involvement, or in the case of the *Vigilance* in 1764, their illegal involvement. Even up until the middle of the nineteenth century a ship coming to grief on the coast of Ceredigion was liable to be plundered by the local population, especially it seems if liquid refreshment was to be found amongst the cargo. Should a vessel avoid being plundered by the local population and the cargo be saved the price of salvage was high with everybody seeming to want a generous payment for their assistance. Even with the numerous newspaper reports and official publications such as the *Admiralty Register of Wrecks* published during the 1850s there is not one wholly reliable source for seeking out details of shipwrecks, each source has strengths, weaknesses and omissions. This book has thus been drawn from a number of sources. During more recent times a small number of books have touched on the subject of shipwrecks in Cardigan Bay. These include Tom Bennett's *Welsh Shipwrecks Vol I and Shipwreck Index of the British Isles, Vol 5 West Coast & Wales* by Richard & Bridget Larn. In addition the excellent journals *Cymru A'r Mor / Maritime Wales* and *Ceredigion* (journal of the Ceredigion Historical Society) have also proved invaluable.

As the author cannot hope to better the eloquent style of the local nineteenth century journalists many accounts of the time have been reproduced verbatim and the source credited. However, place-names have been edited to reflect present day spelling as per the Ordnance Survey. For example, to prevent confusion, and for the sake of consistency, Llanon has been used instead of Llansantfraed (still the name of the parish today), but also used to describe the village itself during the nineteenth century.

Abbreviations

The number of abbreviations used has been kept to a minimum. There are however some that may cause readers confusion and are listed below.
AO = Aberystwyth Observer; CDH = Carnarvon & Denbigh Herald; CN = Cambrian News; CTA = Cardigan & Tivyside Advertiser; grt = gross registered tonnage (this is an indication of the size of a vessel, the term gross is usually used to measure the total permanently enclosed space on a vessel and is usually only used when referring to steam and motor vessels. Other tonnage figures are net tonnage); LL = Lloyds List; SMG = Shipping & Mercantile Gazette.

Acknowledgements

Helen Palmer and the staff of Ceredigion Archives; Michael Freeman, Ceredigion Museum; Robert Baxter, Cumbria Archive Service; Staff of the Guildhall Library, London; David Rimmer, Gwent Record Office; Gwynedd Archives Service; David E Jenkins; Lorena Lord; David Dearborn, Maine Maritime Museum; Numerous members of staff at the National Library of Wales, particularly in the South Reading Room; Staff of Pembrokeshire Record Office; Philip Hocking, Somerset Record Office; Staff at Suffolk Record Office; Dave Taylor, Aldebaran.

CHAPTER 1

The Teifi Estuary and Environs

Judged on the number of known shipwrecks, the Teifi estuary can be seen to be the most treacherous stretch of water on the Ceredigion coast. Indeed, there are bound to be many nineteenth century houses in Cardigan that have had ships timbers incorporated into their construction. One example is the tiller that served as part of a staircase in a house in Greenfield Row. This is now on display at the Cardigan Heritage Centre. It is not poor seamanship that is responsible for these losses but the bar at the entrance to the Teifi. A natural feature, caused by a combination of long-shore drift and the deposition of rocks and stones by the Teifi as it reaches the sea, the bar and river mouth are undergoing constant change and can wrong-foot even experienced sailors. Vessels arriving in good order and calm conditions were able to signal for a pilot to come aboard and navigate the vessel across the bar and through the sandbanks beyond. To a vessel blown in to unfamiliar waters on a storm, possibly at an unfavourable state of the tide and with the Teifi in spate, circumstances were very different and, frequently, tragic. The best they could hope to do was to throw their anchors overboard and pray they would gain a suitable purchase and prevent the vessel being blown ashore. Winds from the northwest were frequently contributory factors to the destruction of ships attempting to navigate their way up the Teifi.

Time has robbed us of many details of the earliest shipwrecks in the district so unfortunately the exact nature and location of wrecks such as the *Samuel* in January 1707, and the *Major Pincke*, in October 1706, have been lost. Both wrecks came to light as the portion of their cargoes salvaged were shipped on in other vessels sailing from Cardigan. The salvaged cargoes were sixty-six barrels of white herring, stockings, feathers and tallow in the case of the *Samuel*, and eleven tons and nineteen hundredweight of tallow in the case of *Major Pincke*.

Once over the bar, the myriad sandbanks were also responsible for the destruction of ships. When *Adolphe* ran aground in 1909, the half-mile of beach between Pen yr Ergyd to Nant-y-ferwig was strewn with onions washed out of her hold. No doubt these were put to use by a grateful local population. In the early part of the twentieth century a number of vessels that came to grief in the Teifi estuary, such as *Ezel* and *John Ewing*, were salvaged by local entrepreneurs.

As well as those vessels subsequently salvaged, there are also a number of narrow escapes which, but for a stroke of luck, would also have graced the pages of this book. One of the most notable of these was the German vessel *Dollart*. On 7th March 1873. *Dollart*, of Detzum (near Hanover), left Cardigan in ballast for Fowey. Upon reaching Dinas Head she encountered heavy seas and a strong south-westerly wind. The master decided to head back to Cardigan and brought up inside Cemaes Head with two anchors and 70 fathoms of chain in seven and a half fathoms of water. She was reached by the hobbler's boat who took the captain's wife ashore and left two men on board to assist the crew. By noon the following day the wind had veered, around to the north-west and the vessel was seen flying signals of distress. The lifeboat was launched and *Dollart* reached after an hour of hard rowing. The master, crew, hobblers and ship's dog were taken off and *Dollart*, by now dragging her anchors, was abandoned to her fate. Eventually, the anchors caught just outside

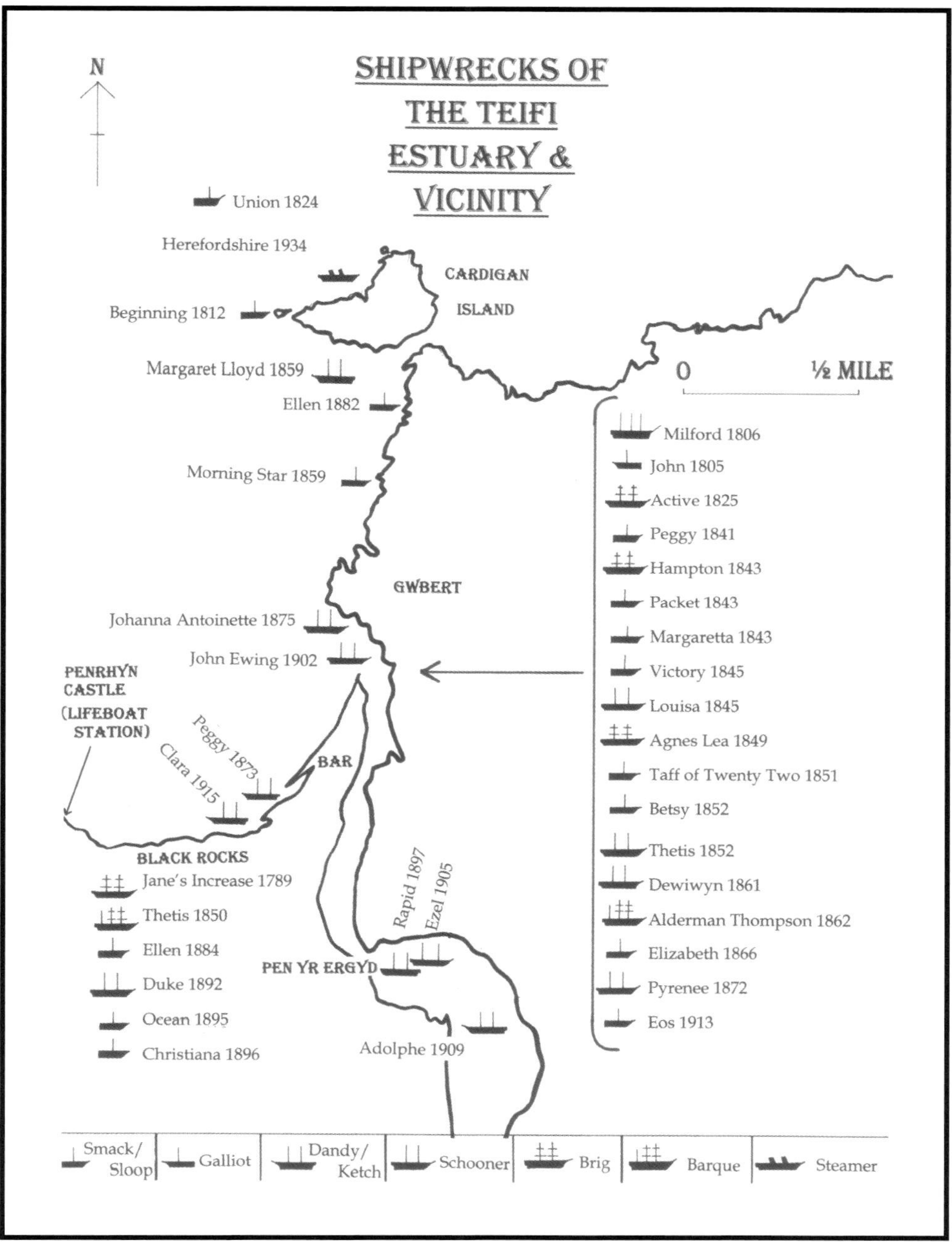

SHIPWRECKS OF THE TEIFI ESTUARY & VICINITY
N
Union 1824
Herefordshire 1934
CARDIGAN ISLAND
Beginning 1812
Margaret Lloyd 1859
Ellen 1882
Morning Star 1859
GWBERT
0
½ MILE
Milford 1806
John 1805
Active 1825
Peggy 1841
Hampton 1843
Packet 1843
Margaretta 1843
Victory 1845
Louisa 1845
Agnes Lea 1849
Taff of Twenty Two 1851
Betsy 1852
Thetis 1852
Dewiwyn 1861
Alderman Thompson 1862
Elizabeth 1866
Pyrenee 1872
Eos 1913
Johanna Antoinette 1875
John Ewing 1902
PENRHYN CASTLE (LIFEBOAT STATION)
Peggy 1873
Clara 1915
BAR
BLACK ROCKS
Jane's Increase 1789
Thetis 1850
Ellen 1884
Duke 1892
Ocean 1895
Christiana 1896
Rapid 1897
Ezel 1905
PEN YR ERGYD
Adolphe 1909
Smack/ Sloop
Galliot
Dandy/ Ketch
Schooner
Brig
Barque
Steamer

the breaking waves. At midday on Sunday, the ninth of March, the wind had abated, and the crew were able to board her. Had the anchors not held where they had *Dollart* would have been forced into the surf and destroyed.

At Cilgerran, further up the Teifi, the slate quarries were in the habit of dumping waste from the slate quarries straight into the river. This caused the river to silt up and in 1851 Captain Washington from the Admiralty commented "In no case have I witnessed anything to be compared with the reckless, wilful destruction of a fine navigable river." Prior to the silting problem the restriction caused by the bar required exceptional tides to enable vessels of over 160 tons to navigate the Teifi. The silting problem prevented the larger vessels seen earlier in the century reaching Cardigan. The railway did not arrive in Cardigan until 1886 and, consequently, small coasting vessels continued to provide an essential and economical service to Cardigan. Inevitably, a number of these vessels are mentioned in this chapter, victims of inclement weather and human error. The last commercial cargo brought into Cardigan was in 1957. In 1981 Cardigan ceased to be a port of registration.

It is perhaps opportune to mention at this point that some of the wrecks detailed in this chapter were technically in Pembrokeshire and not Ceredigion. They have been included here for the sake of completeness.

Convert

Date wrecked 1644
Type of vessel Frigate
Believed to have sunk off Cardigan sometime in 1644. Cardigan Castle was at this time caught up in the English Civil War. The castle was being defended by the Royalists, who were able to retrieve the cannons from the wrecked *Convert* and use them to (unsuccessfully) defend the castle.

John & Ann

Date wrecked 23rd August 1704
Port of registry London
The demise of the *John & Ann* is recorded in the port book for the Port of Cardigan. The vessel is stated as being "wrecked at Cardigan", having been on a voyage from Lisbon. The vessel's master is listed as John Guy. The cargo, listed only because duty was payable, is recorded as "500 oranges and lemons." This seems a very small cargo and probably represents what was salvaged after the vessel was wrecked.

Unknown fishing boats

Date wrecked November 1789
Type of vessel Fishing boats
Three fishing boats belonging to the River Teifi nr Cardigan unfortunately perished in the late storm. Out of twenty eight men which manned the boats, twenty seven were married: twenty widows and fifty six children are the mourners on this occasion. On the same night two other boats were lost at New Quay and the families of eighteen poor men are left to lament their loss.
The Times 17th November 1789

Jane's Increase

Date wrecked November 1789
Built 1782
Type of vessel Brig, 160 tons
Port of registry Whitehaven
The Jane's Increase, Winks of Whitehaven, loaded with mahogany from the Bay of Honduras struck on a ridge of rocks at the mouth of Cardigan Bay, North Wales in the late storm and lost her rudder. In about ten minutes she filled with water and overset: the crew then got upon her broadside. In about half an hour the master died with the cold; and in a few minutes two others of the crew died by the extreme cold (the water continually washing over the hull) and one man was lost in attempting to secure the boat. The remainder kept their miserable station from two in the morning until three in the afternoon when the vessel drove amongst the rocks at the head of the bay and uprighted. Enfeebled by the cold and hunger they with much difficulty crawled up the main rigging and remained there until the water ebbed when they again went upon deck. About nine o'clock two more of these unfortunate men died and at ten o'clock the three survivors Mr Robert White (mate) the boatswain and one man were taken on shore by the neighbouring inhabitants who behaved with the greatest humanity on this

melancholy occasion and by whose assistance all the materials (except the sails) and the cargo are saved.
The Times 01/12/1789

St Johannes
Date wrecked Sept 1800
master Blandon from Liverpool to Falmouth, in ballast, is lost near Cardigan
Lloyds List 13th September 1800

De Jung Jacob
Date wrecked Sept 1800
master O'berg from Dublin to Malaga is on shore near Cardigan
Lloyds List 13th September1800

John
Date wrecked 7th Jan 1805
Built Bridgwater
Type of vessel Galliot, 87 tons
On Monday the 7th inst at 5a.m. the galliot John, Owens master from Liverpool laden with rock salt for Kinsale was driven through stress of weather on Cardigan Bar: fortunately all the hands were saved by the spirited and praiseworthy exertions of the fishermen of St Dogmaels who ventured through the amazing surf at risk of their lives. The sea breaking entirely over the vessel soon rendered her a mere wreck and part came on shore. She had been on the coast of Ireland where an officer [ie a pilot] *was put on board to convey her to her place of destination but experiencing a gale of wind in Bantry Bay she obliged to put to sea with loss of cable and anchor after which she was to drive about for upwards of 20 days, for the last nine days they subsisted principally on potatoes, having no bread left. At the time of her making Cardigan the square sail only remained, all the others being split, her bowsprit carried away, no provisions whatsoever on board and to add to their misfortune the master had one of his ribs broken and his knee-pan* [kneecap] *displaced.*
The Cambrian 13th January 1805

Milford
Date wrecked 3rd December 1806
Built Edgecomb, Mass., 1805
Type of vessel Ship, 214 tons
Port of registry Wiscasset
Setting out from Liverpool with salt and coal for Wilmington, on 23rd November *Milford* had experienced bad weather in the Irish Sea. She was eventually driven on shore on Cardigan Bar, the same day as *Eliza* of Ipswich. *Milford* was described as a total wreck in the press of the day. Her masts, rigging and other salvaged items were offered at auction the following week.

Amphithrite
Date wrecked October 1811
Type of vessel Sloop
Port of Registry Aberystwyth
As with many early shipwrecks details are scant. The only record for the demise of this vessel is in the form of an inquest for Griffith Owen, a seaman aboard the *Amphithrite*, who drowned along with two other men when their

vessel was caught in a gale and wrecked. The body of the unfortunate Griffith Owen was found near Cardigan.

Beginning
Date wrecked 5th March 1812
Type of vessel Sloop
Port of registry Cardigan
The end came for *Beginning* when "in the stress of weather on the 5th March last *[Beginning]* drove and struck upon a certain rock called Silian joining Cardigan Island and was unfortunately wrecked." The Cardigan Gaol Files for this period (from which the above quotation is taken) include inquests into the deaths of the master of the vessel Evan Francis and seaman John Richards. A third anonymous member of the crew was also drowned. *Beginning* was on a voyage from Dundalk to Plymouth at the time and presumably headed into Cardigan for shelter.

Lively
Date wrecked 21st September 1824
Built Aberystwyth, 1807
Type of vessel Sloop, 59 tons
Port of registry Aberystwyth
The sloop *Lively* of Aberystwyth, Evan Doughton master, sailed from her homeport on the Monday 20th of September 1824 for Carmarthen in ballast. The following day a severe gale sprang up and *Lively* foundered off Cardigan, with all the crew saved.

Union
Date wrecked 14th October 1824
Type of vessel Sloop
Port of Registry Aberystwyth
In company with another Aberystwyth sloop *The Twins*, Captain Delahoyd left Neath with a cargo of culm for his home port. As they entered Cardigan Bay the wind increased to gale force claiming first *The Twins* off Strumble Head and shortly afterwards *Union* off Cardigan Head [sic]. Both crews were saved.

Active
Date wrecked 7th Oct 1825
Built Gt Yarmouth, 1795
Type of vessel Brig, 169 tons
Port of registry Whitehaven
Cardigan 08.10.1825 master Johnston from Quebec was driven on shore yesterday during a heavy gale at NW near the entrance of the bar and totally wrecked, the master and two of the crew drowned. Cargo washed out and a great part floated on shore
Lloyds List 8th October 1825

Subsequent newspaper reports listed three of the crew as having drowned. During the following weeks several pieces of pine and oak were washed on shore at Aberystwyth along with carcasses of sheep, cattle and pigs. The timber was believed to be cargo from the *Active* whilst the animal carcasses were from the schooner *Horatia*, lost off St David's Head at the same time.

Peggy

Date wrecked 2nd October 1841
Built 1782
Type of vessel Sloop, 27 tons

An aging 27-ton sloop, *Peggy*, was sailing from Caernarfon to Milford Haven when she was lost on Cardigan Bar on 2nd October 1841.

Hampton

Date wrecked November 1843
Built New Brunswick, 1841
Type of vessel Brig, 136 tons
Port of registry Wicklow

At Cardigan the following vessels came on shore on Saturday. The Hampton, Rowlands from Liverpool for Marseilles, crew saved, cargo expected to be saved. The packet Bristol Trader totally wrecked, crew perished. Two schooners and a sloop, names unknown, sank in the bay.
CDH 04th November1843.

In subsequent Lloyds Registers *Hampton* is listed as having had a new keel and repairs suggesting that she was got off Cardigan Bar having sustained damage. The vessel referred to as the *Bristol Packet* appears to be *Packet* of Cardigan, which ran a regular service between Cardigan and Bristol.

Packet

Date wrecked 25th October 1843
Built Cardigan 1836
Type of vessel Sloop, 33 tons
Port of registry Cardigan

Cardigan - Melancholy shipwrecks, dreadful loss of life. On Saturday week the Cardigan Packet, Evans master was discovered to be on shore in Cardigan Bay, First seen at daybreak, at that time sailors were to be seen clinging to the rigging. The storm increased in violence and the sailors dropped off one by one and were engulfed. No attempt could be made to save them. The crew were Benjamin Bowen (master), David James, John Rees, Thomas Rees and, Thomas Thomas. About ten other vessels ran ashore. The Margaretta of Plymouth (sic) was wholly wrecked and the men lost.
CDH 11th October 1843

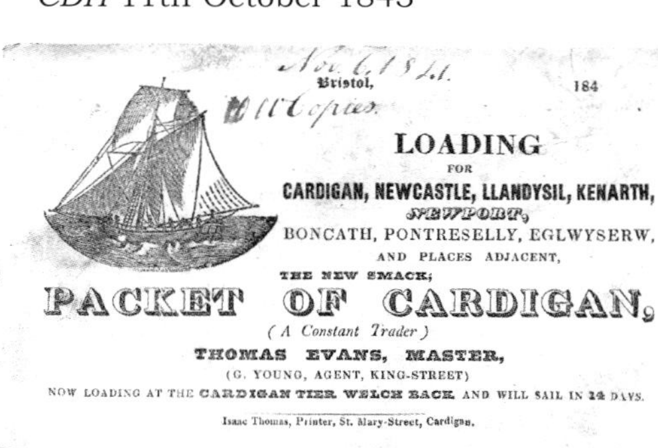

An 1841 advertisement for the services of *'Packet'* of Cardigan (By permission of Llyfrgell Genedlaethol Cymru/National Library of Wales)

Margaretta

Date wrecked 25th October 1843
Type of vessel Smack
Port of Registry Barmouth

The exact circumstances that led to the loss of *Margaretta* on Cardigan Bar can only be guessed at, her demise having taken place during a dark and stormy night with no one to witness the tragedy.

St Dogmaels churchyard has a memorial stone erected in memory of John, Owen and Robert Owen, all from Barmouth of the smack *Margaretta*, which sunk in Cardigan Bay on 25th October 1843.

Victory
Date wrecked 21st December 1845
Type of vessel Sloop
Port of Registry Pembroke
One of two vessels wrecked in the locality on the same day, *Victory* struck Cardigan Bar early on Sunday afternoon, 21st December 1845. Although for most people this was the shortest day of the year, for the crew it was anything but. As the vessel filled with water the crew scampered up the rigging and took to the topmast. They lashed themselves to the mast and waited until the early hours of Monday morning when the conditions had ameliorated sufficiently for the lifeboat to reach them. For most of the sixteen hours during which they had been tied to the mast the sea had been beating over them. On rescue they were described, not surprisingly, as being in a miserable state of suffering.

Margaret Mary
Date wrecked 21st December 1845
Built Aberystwyth, 1842
Type of vessel Smack, 31 tons
Port of registry Aberystwyth
Some five miles further along the Ceredigion coastline, on the same morning as the crew of *Victory* were being rescued, an attentive coastguard observed a masthead protruding from a cave under a high cliff. Proceeding to the spot, he found the wreck of the *Margaret & Mary* of Aberystwyth, along with the corpse of her captain, thirty-six-year old Richard Jones of Borth and a seaman severely bruised but alive. She was carrying a cargo of Limestone from Drogheda in Ireland when caught out by the storm. Captain Richard Jones is buried in Llandre churchyard.

Louisa
Date wrecked Dec 1845
Built Perth, 1840
Type of vessel Schooner, 125 tons
Port of Registry Perth
Cardigan – The Louisa of Perth which was wrecked on the Bar last week has discharged her cargo, which is considerably damaged and she is now brought up to Mr David Owens shipyard to be repaired. Considerable repairs are required according to the Lloyds surveyor and the captains appointed on the survey. We are happy to say that the crew were relieved by the Merchant Seaman's Fund.
Pembrokeshire Herald 2nd January 1846.
Louisa was evidently repaired and still in service 5 years later.

Agnes Lea
Date wrecked 11th January 1849
Built Hwd'n, 1842

Type of vessel Brig, 305 tons
Port of Registry Newcastle

Disastrous Shipwreck on Cardigan Bar and Loss of Lives. *The coast near Cardigan was on Tuesday the 9th inst visited by a tremendous gale and storm, which increased in violence during Wednesday. The hurricane continued without the slightest cessation or abatement during the whole of Wednesday night and on Thursday morning a large vessel was descried in the bay, apparently in distress and making for the entrance to the river. The sea at the time was rolling with terrific violence and the wind blew a perfect hurricane. About 12 o'clock midday the vessel, which proved to be the Agnes Lea, made for the mouth of the river and within an hour ran on the sands of Cardigan Bar when she became instantly unmanageable. A great number of persons assembled on the shore but from the boisterous nature of the sea were unable to render the ill-fated vessel or crew the slightest assistance. Immediately after striking the crew launched the longboat and thirteen persons including the captains wife and infant son got into it for the purpose of getting on shore as the brig was fast breaking up, her entire stern and part of her deck having been washed away. Directly the boat cast off from the vessel a heavy sea struck and the whole thirteen persons were instantly struggling for their lives in the raging ocean. Of this number we regret to state only three reached the shore alive, namely the mate and two seamen. The captain, his wife and child, and seven seamen being drowned. It was only in consequence of superhuman exertions that the survivors were rescued and it is due especially to notice the heroic exertions of Captain George Bowen of St Dogmaels who at the imminent peril of his life seized the mate just as he was sinking and succeeded in saving his life, the two other seamen reached the shore by swimming having the aid of the oars of the boat. It appears directly the boat cast off from the vessel a heavy sea struck, she capsized and that so suddenly the entire crew were thrown under her – the mate had the greatest difficulty in clearing the boat but then swam for the shore and would inevitably have sunk had not Captain Bowen so manfully, and in defiance of such appalling danger swam to his rescue. It appears from the statements of survivors that the brig was from Alexandria laden with wheat, that she sailed from North Shields and was about 500 tons burthen. She arrived from Alexandria about three weeks since at Cork and whilst there the crew with which she had arrived were put off and fresh hands engaged to enable the captain to perform the voyage to Liverpool for which port she left Cork on the Monday previous and whither was bound when the terrible storm arose, during which the vessel started some of her timbers [ie sprung the timbers from their proper position] and becoming nearly waterlogged it was found necessary to head for the first port that*

appeared. The captains wife joined at Cork on the Monday previous and brought with her their infant child, a boy aged about nine months and born during the fathers absence. The infant was washed ashore within a short time after the boat was upset and lived for some minutes. This most dreadful disaster has shed a gloom over the entire town and but one universal feeling exists that it is an imperative necessity which is constantly being manifested: in this instance it is positively asserted by old and experienced mariners that had there been a lifeboat or another available mode of rendering assistance at hand the entire crew might have been saved. The mate states that at the time the captain left the ship he had one hundred pounds in his pocket. The following are the names of the persons drowned captain John Clarence, Elizabeth his wife and their infant son; Michael Tobin, seaman; Charles Thomas, seaman; Henry King, seaman; John Ancross, cook; Francis Pettersen, seaman; Richard and James, two apprentices, one of whom was a nephew of the mate. The names of the survivors are Charles Fortune, chief mate, Timothy Horilton, Thomas Clement and Michael Pierce, seaman. The last mentioned was lashed to the rigging for 24 hrs without clothing or food before he could be got off. The whole of the bodies of those recovered except that of the captain, which has not yet been found.
CDH 27/01/1849

Thetis

Date wrecked 6th February 1850
Type of vessel Barque, 208 tons
Port of registry Limerick
On Wednesday morning during a terrific gale that blew on Tuesday night and Wednesday a large brig was driven on to the bay on the Pembrokeshire side and shortly after striking she went to pieces and it is certain that eleven persons drowned. Two persons are saved, one of who appears to be the captain. The vessel is thought to be Thetis from Limerick but this is not definite, as both men are insensible. There have been 21 persons drowned in two storms at this place within a short period, on each occasion in broad daylight in sight of thousands of their fellow creatures.
C.J. 8th February 1850.

A boat attempted on three separate occasions to row out to *Thetis*, each time with a fresh crew but was beaten back each time. The vessel was under the command of a Captain Donohue. Laden with coal, coopers staves & hoops with a crew of 10 and 2 apprentices she encountered hurricane force winds between 2 and 3 o'clock on Tuesday 5th February 1850. The following morning all her sails were blown away and the vessel left to the fury of the storm. She struck on Cardigan bar at 9 am Wednesday morning. All traces of wreckage had vanished within two hours. At one point the lifeboat was near enough to take a rope from *Thetis* but was knocked back by a big wave before it could do so. Three of the crew made it to shore. John Hayes died shortly afterwards. One other survivor was named as Peter Gilbert. All bodies were subsequently recovered.

Taff of Twenty Two
Date wrecked 29th October 1851
Built Cardiff, 1822
Type of vessel Sloop, 26 tons
Port of registry Cardigan
Lost at the entrance to the Teifi, no further details have come to light.

Betsy
Date wrecked 30th January 1852
Type of vessel Smack, 37 tons
Port of registry Barmouth
Heading for Caernarfon with a cargo of coal from Milford Haven *Betsy* got caught in a vicious north north-westerly storm and tried to head in to Cardigan for shelter. The master and owner, Captain Barrow, was not familiar with the lower reaches of the Teifi. Sadly conditions were too rough to allow a pilot to get aboard. As *Betsy* tried to negotiate the entrance to the Teifi she got caught up in the currents caused by the fresh river water mixing with the warmer seawater. The currents made the small smack unmanageable and she grounded on the bar at a spot known locally as Twm–path-shot. Her plight had been noticed and a boat was launched from the shore and the three crewmen safely rescued. *Betsy* was seen to beat heavily on the bar for sometime until eventually sinking below the waves.

Sussex
Date wrecked 6th November 1852
Built Hastings 1831
Type of vessel Smack, 42 tons
Port of Registry Aberystwyth
Lost on Cardigan Bar, exact circumstances unknown.

Thetis
Date wrecked 22nd December 1852
Built Chepstow 1821
Type of vessel Schooner, 81 tons
Port of registry Cardigan
Cardigan 24.12 [1852] – master Davies of this port from Swansea in crossing the bar on the 22nd struck and sank. The cargo has been got out
LL 28th Dec 1852

Mary
Date wrecked 10th November 1858
Official no. 16120
Built Milford, 1821
Type of vessel Schooner, 55 tons
Port of Registry Cardigan
Lost near Hatling Fach, near Clos-y-graig farm, just to the east of Mwnt. *Mary* was carrying a cargo of Carnarvon slates when she was blown onto the rocks. For many months afterwards her masts were visible at low water and became something of a local landmark.

Morning Star
Date wrecked 25th October 1859
*Official no.*9864
Built Aberystwyth, 1827

Type of vessel Smack, 47 tons
Port of Registry Aberystwyth
This aging smack was lost off Cardigan Head on the 25th October 1859 with the loss of three lives. The bodies of the crew were found at Ceibwr and returned to Aberystwyth. The headstone of the master, Isaac Thomas, and his son was to be found in St Michaels churchyard and can now be seen near the Castle Theatre, Aberystwyth.

Headstone for Isaac Thomas, master of Morning Star and his son Lewis both drowned October 25th 1859

Margaret Lloyd

Date wrecked 25th October 1859
Official no. 8156
Built Aberystwyth, 1854
Type of vessel Dandy, 59 tons
Port of Registry Aberystwyth
This dandy rigged smack became a victim of what came to be known as the "*Royal Charter* Gale." *Royal Charter* foundered on the coast of Anglesey with the loss of five hundred lives in hurricane force winds that blew over a large part of Britain on the night of 25th October 1859. *Margaret Lloyd* was one of 133 vessels lost in British waters in the space of this one night when what started off as a gale rapidly evolved first into a storm and swiftly a hurricane. Owned and commanded by Captain William Lloyd the younger of Aberystwyth *Margaret Lloyd* was carrying a cargo of slates. Her loss caused particular anguish in Aberystwyth. For some three hours, between seven and ten o'clock she was seen to be tacking back and forth in the bay about a mile or so from shore and evidently in great distress. As no light was being shown at the harbour she was unable to locate the entrance. The harbour master was informed of the circumstances by both members of the captain's family and by other bystanders but neglected to take any action. Consequently, *Margaret Lloyd* had to take her chances elsewhere as the gale increased in intensity into a storm and then a hurricane. Forced by the hurricane descending from the north to head down the coast, *Margaret Lloyd* and her crew of four perished when the vessel ran out of luck and sank near Cardigan Island.
The first inkling that the vessel had gone down was the site of two masts that could be seen above water three hundred or so metres east south east of Cardigan Island. Despite some

initial confusion (caused by the finding of part of an oar with *Credo* branded thereon) the vessel was subsequently identified as *Margaret Lloyd*.

Subsequently, the incident made headlines in the national maritime press. The town's maritime community, outraged at the needless loss of life took action to make sure that such neglect could not happen again.

Dewiwyn

Date wrecked 21st January 1861
*Official no.*1083
Built Porthmadog
Type of vessel Schooner, 49 ton
Port of registry Caernarfon
Lifeboat services - Cardigan. *During a heavy ground sea and the wind blowing fresh from the NW the schooner Dewi Wyn from Porthmadog was stranded on a bank in Cardigan Bay on Monday. As soon as the signals of distress indicating the perilous position of the ship were seen the lifeboat of the National Lifeboat Institution was manned and launched. On approaching the wreck the sea could be seen to be breaking completely over her: but after some difficulty the schooners crew of four and four hovellers* [hobblers] *were taken off by the lifeboat and safely brought on shore. The lifeboat has been some years on station but never yet had the opportunity to save life. It is however evident that in her absence on the present occasion the lives of eight men would have been imperilled.*
CDH 23rd February 1861

Alderman Thompson

Date wrecked October 1862
*Official no.*24663
Built Sunderland, 1840
Type of vessel Barque, 272 tons
Port of Registry Sunderland
Cardigan Bar. On Sunday last and during the following Monday a terrible gale prevailed in this neighbourhood and it is feared that much damage has been sustained. A fine barque named the Alderman Thompson of Sunderland, commanded by Captain Agae freighted with a large cargo of timber from Quebec for Mr John S Williams of Cardigan, merchant while attempting to enter the mouth of the river ran onto the bank at Cardigan Bar and soon became a wreck. By great exertions the whole of the crew were saved. Both ship and cargo are fully insured. A heavy gale prevailed during Sunday night and Monday last and the vessel was carried by the force of the waves into a more favourable position.
The Cambrian 24th Oct 1862

Elizabeth

Date wrecked 23rd March 1866
Type of vessel Smack
Port of registry Cardigan
Attempting to reach her home port with a general cargo from Bristol in a southerly gale, the smack *Elizabeth* had the misfortune for her jib sheet to be wrenched from its cleat by the strength of the wind, just as the foresail was required to help steer her over Cardigan bar. She struck the sandbank and was soon being

pounded by waves that washed clean over the vessel. The ship's boat was swamped and the crew retreated to the rigging where their plight was soon noticed. As might be expected, word spread and spectators gathered to watch the drama unfold. Amongst these were four young men (John Evans and George Richards of Capel Dogwell; George Richards of High Street, St Dogmaels and John Thomas of Cwminns). On the way, the four would-be spectators called in at the Poppit House for a strengthening glass of home brewed beer. Instead of serving them a reviving glass of bitter the landlady told them to hurry up and get along to the lifeboat station as the crew were short. The lifeboat was launched with the four young men managing the oars. The lifeboat gained the stern of *Elizabeth* and the six crewmen were able to scramble down into the lifeboat. Last to leave the stricken vessel was a local pilot, David Morris, nicknamed David Jos. He was remembered for having first thrown his precious umbrella into the boat before scrambling in himself. Some thirty years later the *Cardigan & Tivyside Advertiser* noted that David Jos was never to be seen without an umbrella.

James

Date wrecked 3rd February 1867
*Official no.*10278
Built Lawrenny, 1844
Type of vessel Schooner, 70 tons
Port of Registry Cardigan
The schooner James, Evans sank off Carrigduon [Black Rocks] *within the bar yesterday. She is laden with culm from Hook in the Milford River. She crossed the bar on Saturday evening and struck the south side but went towards the north side and lies on the beach accessible at low water.*
SMG 5th February 1867

James was successfully salvaged and after various repairs, a reduction in her tonnage and a new deck continued in service along the Welsh coast.

Primrose

Date wrecked 27th Nov 1870
*Official no.*8853
Type of vessel Smack, 51 tons
Port of registry Aberystwyth
Foundering of a smack. Narrow escape of the crew. *About 7pm Sunday evening Nov 27th the smack Primrose belonging to this port, Capt James Jones was on passage with a cargo bound for Newcastle. Some ten miles out of Aberporth the vessel sprang a leak. The crew which consisted of three men and captain Jones set to pumping and continued to do so all night. About 9am next morning when they had found the water was gaining on them not withstanding their efforts and that it was useless to stay any longer on board. In an exhausted state they took to the boat and made off through a heavy sea. It was fortunate they had taken this course of action for the smack sank before they had gone a*

hundred yards. The unfortunate crew for a long time struggled through the tempestuous seas and would have all been drowned had not an Aberaeron steamer [SS Cadwgan] seen them and picked them up. They were landed safely at New Quay.
CN 3rd December 1870

Pyrenee
Date wrecked 11th Nov 1872
Official no 11199
Built Aberaeron, 1856
Type of vessel Schooner, 39 tons
Port of registry Plymouth
Loss of a Schooner with all Hands
During the severe gale, which visited the coast of Cardigan Bay on Monday, the schooner Pyrenees (sic), formerly owned by Mrs Gwen Evans of this town, but now the property of a gentleman from Exeter was making for Cardigan with a cargo of salt when she was driven ashore in the mouth of the bar and became a total wreck. The crew, five in number unfortunately perished. The bodies of two or three have already been washed ashore. The calamity has cast a gloom over the town of Cardigan and the neighbourhood.
CDH 16th November 1872

Shipwreck & loss of life on Cardigan Bar *Sunday night last will long be remembered on the western coast board for the terrific gale, which raged from the northwest, lashing the sea into a mass of foaming billows. On Monday morning pieces of wreck were observed on the sand on the Pembrokeshire side of the bar and on further search the two masts were discovered floating where the vessel was supposed to have struck, about 20 yards from the old wreck. The bodies of the crew, three in number, natives of Devon and Cornwall have been washed ashore and will be interred in St Dogmaels Churchyard tomorrow (sat). The vessel proved to be the Pyrenee, Captain May, previously of Aberystwyth.*
CTA 15th November 1872

Three of the crew were buried in the same grave in St Dogmaels churchyard. Their gravestone reads as follows:
MAY, Stephen, of Foeck, Cornwall. Master of the *Pyrenee.*
HICKS, William of Devonport. Mate of the Pyrenee.
CROSS, John of Bristol. Boy on the *Pyrenee.*
Remembered died 11th Nov 1872, when the ship was wrecked on Cardigan Bay.

Rachel
Date wrecked 6th October 1873
*Official no.*16140
Built Cei Bach, 1836
Type of vessel Sloop, 25 tons
Port of registry Cardigan
Foundered off Cardigan whilst sailing from Llangranog to Milford in ballast. Sand was being used as ballast but had not been properly stowed. When

the vessel started to take in water the pumps were used but they eventually became choked with the sand.

Peggy

Date wrecked 19th October 1873
Official no. 16431
Built Chester, 1836
Type of vessel Dandy, 35 tons
Port of Registry Cardiff

The sloop *Peggy*, owned and commanded by Mr Daniel Howells of St Dogmaels, arrived off Cardigan on the 19th of October 1873. Carrying a cargo of culm from Swansea to Cardigan, her journey had been interrupted by bad weather, forcing her to shelter in Milford Haven for three days. On reaching the Teifi estuary she anchored waiting for the tide. In the meantime the wind shifted to the north-northwest and a further anchor had to be deployed as the wind grew in strength. The sloop started to labour heavily, and a red lamp was hoisted as a signal of distress. A local farmer saw the signal, saddled his horse, and rode to St Dogmaels coastguard station to report the matter. One anchor cable parted shortly after the red lamp was raised and the vessel started to drag the remaining anchor. Despite being four members short the lifeboat was launched and reached the stricken vessel at about 7am and the crew taken off *Peggy* just as she approached the breakers. At 8.30 a.m. the second cable parted and the vessel drove ashore. Once the tide had receded, the cargo was unloaded and the vessel stripped of anything of value. The following night the vessel went to pieces.

Alberta

Date wrecked 7th November 1875
Official no. 29301
Built Aberystwyth, 1861
Type of vessel Schooner, 90 tons
Port of registry Cardigan

Owned by James Walker, a Glasgow merchant, *Alberta* had been launched at Aberystwyth in 1861. Bound from Glasgow to Cardiff with a cargo of gas coal, she left Glasgow at 5am on 6th November 1875. Heavy seas had washed away her headgear, causing her to put into Belfast for repairs. She sailed from Belfast on the Monday morning and sighted the South Bishops lighthouse, off the coast of Ramsey Island, on Saturday morning. It was about this time that the wind shifted to the south-west. At eight o' clock the next morning the master decided to aim for Fishguard Roads. At 5 am on Sunday morning the wind shifted to the north-west and started blowing a gale. On trying the pumps the crew found she was taking in water. By this time the vessel was 35miles north east of the South Bishop lighthouse. The crew continued to work the 2 pumps, but the water was gaining fast. When the vessel was 7 miles from Cardigan the crew insisted on the captain running the ship towards the shore as they were on a lee shore with night approaching. They aimed to beach her as soon as possible. By this time there was 3 feet of water in the hold. The captain aimed her towards the stretch of beach between Cei Bach and the lifeboat shed. The ship closed fast and drove up on the rocks, healing inwards with the yard arms overhanging the rocks. The crew slid down the mast on to the rocks, closely followed by the captain (William Finch from St Dogmaels). All were off the vessel in less than 20 minutes. The vessel broke up soon afterwards. The vessel was valued at £620 but was insured for only £540. The cargo was valued at £150. As the vessel rounded Cardigan Head at 4pm on the Sunday the coastguards had noted that the wind from the NNW had attained hurricane force and that the hull of *Alberta* was completely submerged in the surf.

Johanna Antoinette

Date wrecked 19th November 1875
Type of vessel Schooner, 150 tons
Port of Registry Gravenhage
Older readers will be familiar with the Ealing comedy *Whisky Galore* which tells the story of a ship carrying a cargo of whisky that becomes wrecked on a remote Scottish island. The wreck of the *Johanna Antoinette* is very definitely Ceredigion's answer to *'Whisky Galore'*, though in this case the cargo was Dutch gin, not Scottish whisky. Some of this gin was still being unearthed in the vicinity half a century later. The story is best told as it appeared in the *Cardigan & Tivyside Advertiser:*

Casualty in the Bay. *At 4.30 pm on the 18th of November a vessel was observed by the coastguard coming to anchor in the bay evidently in distress near the bar. The wind was blowing heavily from the WSW the tide being one hour flood. The vessel being in distress the rocket apparatus was got ready and the horses prepared. Also the chief boatman and crew were put on alert in case the wind veered to the north. At 6 am on Friday morning the wind shifted to the northwest and the vessel started to drive on to the bar. The apparatus was started and the first rocket fired from near Glan-y-mor at 6.30am. The vessel was by now ashore. Four rockets were discharged but none could reach the stricken vessel so the lifeboat was launched and the five crew taken off by 7.30 am. An hour and a half later the vessel struck on the worst part of the bar losing her rudder and sustaining severe damage to her bottom. She proved to be the Johanna Antoinette registered at Gravenhage sailing from Rotterdam to Lisbon with a general cargo, mainly gin. The coastguards boarded her and tried every means to save her. At low tide the cargo was unloaded to the warehouse of D G Davies, Lloyds agent for the port. A temporary rudder was rigged and the vessel towed to the Netpool at St Dogmaels where an examination revealed that the damage suffered was such that she was not worth repairing. Mr Hegarty, the chief boatman was singled out for praise for his contribution.*

The story has a sequel, also from the *Cardigan & Tivyside Advertiser* of 28th January 1927:

Last week Mr Tom Williams, Tyrffin, Gwbert found in the sand on the burrows a stone jar with the capsule and cork intact which contained a small quantity of Holland Gin. This brings to mind the wreck of the Johanna Antoinette. It is said that for some months afterwards that whatever short was ordered in local bars gin was served. It is also said that farms in the local district were also well stocked with mothers ruin for a long time after. During the construction of the new road to Gwbert dozens of bottles of gin were dug up on the burrows.

Cardigan.

For further particulars apply to the Auctioneer, at his Offices, at Cardigan.

Cardigan, Dec. 9, 1875.

PORT OF CARDIGAN.

Unreserved Sale of a Dutch Schooner.

TO BE SOLD BY AUCTION (for the benefit of the concerned), on Wednesday, December 15th, 1875, at St. Dogmells, at 12 o'clock (noon) precisely, the HULL of the SCHOONER

"JOHANNA ANTOINETTE,"

Of St. Gravenhage (Holland), as she may then lie; 150 Tons burthen, or thereabouts, & built of Oak, lately stranded on Cardigan Bar; together with her

STORES AND MATERIALS,

Consisting of complete suit of good Sails, Spars, Cordage, Anchors and Chains, Blocks, &c., which will be sold in suitable Lots,

Also, will be SOLD immediately afterwards, 140 kegs of Pearl Barley and 27 bolts of Canvass, slightly damaged by salt water, being part of the Cargo of the said vessel.

TERMS—CASH.

For further particulars apply to

T. T. JACKSON, Esq.,
Consular and Underwriters' Agency
Offices, Milford Haven,

THE

An advertisement for the sale of what remained of the *Johanna Antoinette*, from the *Cardigan & Tivyside Advertiser*, 1875 .

Dispatch

Date wrecked 22nd July 1878
Type of vessel Sloop
Port of Registry Cardigan

Thomas Davies, a draper of Anchor House, Cardigan, was sailing his sloop *Dispatch* in the bay with a large press of sail but no ballast. The vessel capsized four miles north west of Cardigan Bar. Thomas Davies was engulfed by the sails and nearly dragged under. All three aboard were rescued after half an hour clinging to the keel. The boat was abandoned and went to pieces near Mwnt.

Ellen

Date wrecked 7th September 1884
Official no. 16414
Built Liverpool, 1808
Type of vessel Smack, 27 tons
Port of Registry Milford Haven

This smack served Cardigan well for many years bringing in cargoes of coal. *Ellen* is the only vessel in this book to have been wrecked twice. The first incident took place during a gale from the north north-west on first November 1882 when *Ellen*, under Captain John Rees of Milford, was seen flying signals of distress in Cardigan Bay. She was in ballast and seen to be rolling heavily. When seen by coastguard officers she was deemed to be in imminent danger of going ashore on the rocks. The lifeboat was launched from Penrhyn Castle and the crew "showed self denying heroism by the ready manner they plied the boat to the rescue." The crew of three were taken aboard the lifeboat and landed safely. Nothing could be done for the vessel, which was left to the mercy of the waves. Afterwards the vessel ran aground near Cardigan Island in a forlorn state but not seriously damaged.

Two years later, *Ellen* was not so lucky. *Ellen* anchored at the mouth of the Teifi. A gale from the west north-west blew up and her anchors started to drag putting the vessel in imminent danger of being blown onto the Black Rocks. The lifeboat was called out and all aboard rescued by lifeboat. Shortly after her cable parted and the vessel drove ashore becoming a total wreck. Had the gale not abated soon afterwards it is quite likely that the Norwegian brigantine *Unda* also anchored at the mouth of the Teifi would have followed *Ellen* onto the rocks, her anchors already having been dragged for 150 yards.

Reliance

Date wrecked 11th October 1891
Official no. 49503
Built Perth, 1865
Type of vessel Schooner, 86 tons
Port of Registry Wexford
Local rivalries are not uncommon in maritime communities. In this instance the *Cardigan & Tivyside Advertiser* seemed all too happy to fan the flames of rivalry with criticism of the neighbouring lifeboat at Newport, Pembrokeshire.

Shipwreck in Cardigan Bay. Gallant conduct of Volunteers in the Newport Lifeboat. *On Monday night last, about 11o'clock, the attention of the inhabitants of Newport [Pembrokeshire] and the adjoining district was drawn by flares burnt on board to the perilous position of a vessel in the bay apparently disabled. The signals of distress were speedily answered by rocket from the shore and the alarm signal to assemble the crew of the lifeboat Clevedon stationed at the mouth of the Newport River, was fired. Our readers will remember we noticed the arrival of the boat last week at her station after receiving a thorough overhauling and been fitted up with the latest improvements; there was some difficulty there, it appears, in getting the boat round from Cardigan as there was a cupful of a Northwester blowing. On Monday night last, a similar difficulty seemed to have existed as it was sometime before a crew could be got together and even at the last moment the boat had to be put off to the rescue with six only of the regular crew on board out of fifteen, the remainder being made up of volunteers, and some of them landsmen, including Mr J D E Williams, son of Dr Williams of Parrog House, an apprentice with Mr Lewis Evans, chemist, Cardigan who was home for his holidays and was one of the first to volunteer. After a considerable delay the lifeboat was got out, but owing to her unpreparedness, the state of the tide, and the unsuitable position in which the boathouse is situated, it was half past four, according to the story of the captain of* *the distressed vessel before she got alongside. The vessel proved to be the 'Reliance' of Wexford, 45 tons register, bound to Newport, (Monmouthshire) in ballast, with a crew of four men, but the mate had unfortunately jumped overboard previously to try and reach a barque, which bore down to them in the bay, and was drowned. Having rescued the three men, the lifeboat attempted to reach Newport, but was driven by the force of the gale out into the bay & after much exposure managed to cross Cardigan bar, landing at St Dogmaels where they were received by Mr Buckham, the chief officer of coastguards and every assistance rendered them and the shipwrecked crew. The names of the lifeboat crew who effected this gallant rescue are as follow: - Members of the regular crew- Capt Thomas, coxswain, John Stephens, W J Griffiths, W Lewis, Daniel Thomas, and John Laugharne; the volunteers were Capt W Davies, second coxswain, Daniel Davies, Wm Davies, Clement Davies, Capt Llewellyn Davies, Capt D Evans, (brother of the postmaster of Cardigan), J D E Williams, James Thomas, and William James, the whole of whom are worthy of the highest praise for their humane and plucky conduct. This is not the first time, we are informed, the Newport lifeboat crew have been found wanting. There may of course be circumstances connected therewith, which may explain matters, but it appears certain that the sooner the management and position of the Newport lifeboat is seen to the better for all. An attempt was made on Tuesday night by the steam trawler, the Little Malta to tow the lifeboat back to Newport, but the weather off Cemaes Head was too rough for the small steamer and both had to return, but the Clevedon was towed down by the Sea Flower on Wednesday evening. The dismasted vessel was brought safely up to Cardigan, where she now lies, the same evening by the Little Malta. The following is* ***The Captains narrative*** *Captain Hutchinson, master of the Reliance, gives us the following narrative: - we left Wexford for Newport (Mon) in ballast on the 6th instant and at 9 pm sighted the Bishop's lighthouse, there being at the time a strong breeze from the south, the wind rapidly increasing. Early on Monday morning, the 7th instant the vessel was about 15 miles to the north west of the Bishops with a strong south-westerly gale blowing. About 2.15 am the jib-boom was carried away, the forestay directly afterwards sharing the same fate, the foremast going by the board soon afterwards, followed by the mainmast, the latter carrying away with it the winch and bulwarks on the lee side. About 6a.m. they sighted a barque, which he took to be a Norwegian, about seven miles to the southward; also a steamer, thought to be the Jane Bacon of Liverpool. He hoisted a signal of distress, when the barque bore down on them throwing three life buoys over the side. On seeing this, the mate of the Reliance (named James Breen) jumped overboard, but missing the lifebuoys was drowned, his body at once being washed out of sight. The barque then reached away to the*

northwards and the steamer sighted rendered the exhausted crew no assistance. The distressed vessel then made her way as best she could in crippled state to Fishguard Bay, where she dropped anchor about 11pm, and burnt flares to attract attention, which were answered from the shore by rockets, the Newport lifeboat Clevedon coming alongside at 4.30a.m. on Tuesday morning, and taking off the remaining crew of three men and we were safely landed at St Dogmaels at 6.30a.m.
CTA 11/10/1889

Duke
Date wrecked 9th December 1892
Official no. 24117
Built Runcorn, 1888
Type of vessel Schooner, 55 tons
Port of Registry Wicklow
Wreck in Cardigan Bay. *A frightful gale was experienced along the west coast last evening and early this (Fri) morning the sea in Cardigan Bay was running mountains high. The gale was encountered to its fullest extent by the schooner Duke, of Wicklow, which was on passage from Runcorn to Cardigan with a cargo of coal consigned to the Cardigan Brickworks Company. The schooner arrived in the bay about 12 o'clock last night and about 4.15 she was observed to be firing signals of distress which were at once answered by the star rocket from the lifeboat station at Penrhyn Castle. The crew of the boat were speedily in attendance and under the charge of the coxswain Mr David Rees she was at once launched to the rescue of the crew of 3 men. As far as we can learn in the short time since the occurrences the vessel was driven by the wind, and the tide rising she took the rocks close to the Black Rocks near Cemaes Head in a very dangerous position. The rocket apparatus was at once put into requisition, a rocket being fired over the vessel and the hawser caught by the crew, but the lifeboat coming up at the same time it was let go and the men safely landed at the station about 8 o'clock. The schooner, which is of 120 tons burden, is likely to become a complete wreck*
CTA 09/12/1892

Cupid
Date wrecked 11th November 1894
Official no. 51264
Built Jersey, 1865
Type of vessel Schooner, 82tons
Port of Registry Falmouth
It was not the dangers at the entrance to the Teifi that accounted for the *Cupid*, but rather the sandbanks in the lower reaches of the Teifi. *Cupid* was carrying a cargo of guano from London for the Cardigan Mercantile Company when tragedy struck. No account of the wreck appears in the local newspapers, only a letter from Captain William Richards of the *Cupid* thanking Mrs Williams of the Gwbert Hotel for the hospitality received after the sinking of their vessel. The following week the Cardigan Mercantile Company Ltd took out an advertisement in the *Cardigan & Tivyside Advertiser* to reassure their

customers that a duplicate cargo [of fertiliser] had been ordered.

Although the prognosis from the local sea-faring community for *Cupid* was one of doom and gloom, aided by inclement weather conditions - giving her the appearance of an iceberg - *Cupid* still had one lifeline. This came in the form of Mr Bailey of the Cardigan Engineering Works, a man with experience of working in far bigger ports than Cardigan. After removing some 70 tons of cargo, he installed a boiler and engine to power a centrifugal pump capable of discharging 1000 gallons of water per minute. This enabled the vessel to be raised from the riverbed. Following temporary caulking she was brought alongside the Quay in Cardigan, eventually being taken out of the water for repair. This was the first time, but would not be the last, that such a feat would be performed at Cardigan.

Ocean

Date wrecked 2nd October 1895
Official no. 9240
Built Aberaeron, 1827
Type of vessel Smack, 33 tons
Port of Registry Cardigan
The great heat of the latter part of last week and beginning of this week came to an end on Tuesday when the atmosphere cooled and a terrific storm arose on the south and west coasts. Soon after midnight on Tuesday the smack Ocean owned by Mr Evan Jenkins, Pentre Arms, Llangrannog, anchored a mile outside Cardigan Bar in ballast so as to be ready to enter Cardigan by the morning tide to lay up for the winter. The wind freshened and at 2am a terrific gale arose from the north-west. The vessel showed signals of distress for half an hour but received no response from the signal station so the crew - Captain Daniel Davies and the mate – took to their boat, landing at 3am. Soon afterwards the vessels cable parted and she went ashore on the Pembrokeshire side of the bay known as the Black Rocks and smashed to splinters.
CTA 4th October1895

Christiana

Date wrecked 22nd September 1896
Official no. 18735
Built Pembroke, Pembroke Dock, 1857
Type of vessel Smack, 25 tons
Port of Registry Cardigan
Christiana, also owned by Mr Evan Jenkins of the Pentre Arms, Llangrannog, had a close shave in September 1892 when she became stranded on Cardigan Bar. This time she left Cardigan for Goodwick with a cargo of bricks. When some two miles off Newport she decided to turn back due to the high seas running. She reached the shelter of Cardigan at 3pm and anchored three-quarters of a mile off the lifeboat station, throwing two anchors out in case the first anchor dragged. She was then found to be taking water fast and flew signals of distress. At 3.55pm the signal rocket was fired by Penrhyn Castle and the crew of the lifeboat summoned. The lifeboat reached the

vessel by 5pm and rescued the crew. Subsequently *Christiana*'s anchors parted and she was driven ashore on the Black Rocks and totally wrecked. As with many of the vessels wrecked at the entrance to the Teifi, a gale was blowing at the time from the northwest.

Rapid

Date wrecked 12th February 1897
*Official no.*10869
Built Lawrenny, 1821
Type of vessel Ketch, 48 tons
Port of Registry Bridgwater

Rapid was another vessel engaged to carry a cargo for the Cardigan Mercantile Company, this time manure from Dublin. The arrangement was that she was to be towed up the Teifi to Cardigan by the steam trawler *Little Malta*. Shortly after being taken in tow the heavy ground swell snapped the hawser and *Rapid* went ashore on the Cardiganshire side of the bar, presumably near Pen yr Ergyd. A second hawser was attached but *Little Malta* was unable to pull *Rapid* off the beach. The vessel soon became a total wreck, the cargo and stores sold off the next day by William Woodward, auctioneer.

Hannah

Date wrecked 28th January 1901
Official no. 52884
Built Conway, 1865
Type of vessel Schooner
Port of Registry Preston

The site of a dismasted schooner being blown across the bay in an easterly direction on a blustery January morning was reason enough to summon the local lifeboat crew. The launch was delayed because the coxswain was unwilling to set sail until enough experienced crew were available. The matter was resolved, and at midday the lifeboat set off in pursuit of the stricken vessel. By this time she was about to ground on Mwnt beach. Due to the sea conditions the lifeboat was unable to venture into Mwnt and headed off in the direction of Aberporth. On stranding at Mwnt the vessel was ascertained to be the *Hannah*, registered in Preston, in ballast and bereft of any crew. The finding of a piece of rope hanging from the bow was regarded as evidence that the crew had abandoned ship, and the vessel had been taken in tow by another vessel.

Hannah had set sail from Wexford, bound for Newport, when she was overtaken by very stormy weather. Encountering mountainous seas, and in a sinking state, she had signalled her distress to a passing vessel, the steamer *Moorhen* of the Cork Steamship Company. The crew were evacuated and later landed at Dun Laoghaire. An attempt to tow the *Hannah* to Waterford was made but, as surmised, the rope had broken and *Hannah* was left to the elements, washing up at Mwnt the following day. The local coastguard then mounted a round-the-clock guard on the wreck. As this was the only wreck in living memory to have taken place at Mwnt the subsequent auction a fortnight later engendered a great deal of local interest and seems to have taken place in a carnival atmosphere. The hull of the vessel was sold to Mr Thomas, Plas, Aberporth.

John Ewing

Date wrecked 25th March 1902
Official no. 56790
Built Whitehaven, 1867
Type of vessel Schooner, 116 tons
Port of Registry Aberystwyth

On Monday night last was added another disaster near Cardigan Bar, so many of which are already dotted on the map of the Lifeboat Institution; and in most of which the Cardigan lifeboat has been instrumental in saving life. The facts of the case may be gleaned from the following narrative: -

On Sunday morning the schooner 'John Ewing' of Carnarvon, Capt. Hughes, arrived in the bay from London with a cargo of manure for the Cardigan Mercantile Co. and Mr Thomas Thomas, Plas, Aberporth. Being unable to obtain a pilot, the Capt. endeavoured to bring the vessel up the river himself, but she went aground on the banks close to the bar on the Pembrokeshire side. On Monday morning she floated, and passing over the bar into the bay she dropped her anchor between Gwbert and the Lifeboat House, the Capt. going up to Cardigan on business. The weather was threatening all day, the wind blowing in the morning from the South, which, in the afternoon, veered to the Northwest, the wind rising at the same time to almost a hurricane. Hearing of the danger to the vessel, Mr William Joseph Hon. Sec. of the local lifeboat telephoned to the coxswain to be on the watch, and it is no doubt to his forethought that the crew were enabled to be gathered as quickly as they did.

The vessel was closely watched and observing the vessel dragging her anchors, the sea having by this time become terrific in its violence, the alarm rocket was fired from Penrhyn Castle at 7.50 p.m., the lifeboat being so promptly launched as to be afloat at 8.25, only 35 minutes having elapsed. The vicinity of the vessel was reached at about 9 o'clock when it was found she was dragging toward the bar, her anchors being unable to hold her. Finding, owing to the heavy seas and wind, that it was impossible to board the vessel and save the crew of four, Capt. Hughes being then in the lifeboat returning to the ship, the coxswain resolved if possible, to throw a line on board; this, fortunately he succeeded in doing and a rope and lifebelts having been passed to the vessel , the crew were saved as one by one they threw themselves into the sea and were dragged into the lifeboat, which, having effected her purpose, returned to the station at 10.15 p.m. where the shipwrecked crew were landed in an exhausted state, and kindly treated.

The vessel was then blown over the bar and stranded between the Perch and Glan-y-mor Farm, near the same spot as the 'Mouse' some time since. This is the maiden attempt of the new coxswain of the lifeboat Mr Thomas Bowen to save life from shipwreck, and he is to be heartily congratulated on his success, the rescue being carried out most pluckily in the face of the heavy sea running. The 'John Ewing' belongs to two sisters, The Misses Parry and is not insured. On Tuesday morning the ship was under water, the mast only being visible, but the tide left her high and dry. The cargo was insured. On Thursday morning she lay in the same position and it is anticipated that she will become a total wreck.
CTA 28th March 1902

Despite being sunk with only her masts visible this was not the end for *John Ewing.* Financed by wine merchant David Davies, Mr Bailey the engineer was on hand to raise her. Following repairs she was re-registered at Cardigan and lasted until 1922.

Ezel

Date wrecked 1st October 1905
Official no. 68146
Built Cardiff, 1873
Type of vessel Schooner, 140 tons
Port of Registry Cardiff
In what seems an already familiar story the three-masted Cardiff schooner *Ezel* was bringing a cargo of manure to Cardigan for the Vale of Tivy Co-operative Society on 1st October 1905. After negotiating the perch, she struck on Pen Yr Ergyd. As the tide receded, the sand was washed away from under her stern, which due to the lack of support underneath, became strained and damaged. Her owners were forced to write her off and she was sold as she lay on 21st October for £55 to the above-mentioned Mr David Davies who also purchased the cargo for £1. Mr Davies was obviously emboldened by his successful venture with *John Ewing* and was a man with an eye for a bargain. *Ezel* was repaired over a period of eighteen months, and re-registered at Cardigan in July 1907. Mr Davies' faith in *Ezel* was more than amply rewarded as she continued to trade until 8th September 1917 when she was captured by a German U-boat and sunk by gunfire in the English Channel without loss of life.

Anne

Date wrecked 26th October 1906
*Official no.*10655
Built Conwy, 1841
Type of vessel Sloop, 27 tons
Port of registry Beaumaris
Just before 10 am on a Sunday morning, the look out at Penrhyn Castle saw signals of distress four miles off Cardigan Island. Rockets summoned the St.Dogmaels lifeboat crew and the lifeboat *Elizabeth Austin* launched. The vessel *Anne* was reached about 12.30 pm but had drifted a further eight miles. The crew

of two were exhausted after pumping all night. The sails had been blown away, the rudder washed away and

Ezel stranded on Pen Yr Ergyd at the mouth of the Teifi, 1905. (By permission of Llyfrgell) Genedlaethol Cymru/National Library of Wales)

the crew had used up all her oil showing signals of distress. The vessel was left in a sinking state and thought to have gone down about 3.30 pm. The lifeboat *Elizabeth Austin* returned about 4.30 pm. The sea was choppy in the extreme rather than tempestuous with a strong SW wind and squalls. The *Anne* was owned by David Luke of Newport, Pembrokeshire, and was not insured. The vessel had left Cardigan the previous fortnight on another voyage and was noted then as being leaky. This was to have been her last voyage. She was carrying culm from Milford Haven to Newport, Pembrokeshire. Samuel Griffiths, who four months previously had been in charge of the Newport smack *Mary Ann* that sank off Fishguard, commanded *Anne* on this occasion.

Little Malta

Date wrecked 1st November 1906
*Official no.*91659
Built Port Glasgow, 1887
Type of vessel Steamship, 18grt
Port of Registry Cardigan
Frequently used to tow sailing vessels up the Teifi, *Little Malta* sank opposite Cardigan gasworks. She was raised some six weeks later and was eventually broken up at Cardigan in April 1911.

Adolphe

Date wrecked 20th August 1909
Type of vessel Ketch
With their berets, bicycles and strings of onions, Sioni Winwns, the travelling Breton onion salesmen, were a feature of Welsh life for much of the twentieth century. Coming in August each year from Roscoff and Saint-Pol-de-Leon they would stay for up to six months stringing and selling their onions. French vessels would sail right up to the quayside at Cardigan to unload these precious cargoes. However after the demise of the *Adolphe*, below, it seems there would have been slim pickings for Sioni Winwns around Cardigan for a few months !
Waterlogged. *On Friday afternoon last the French ketch Adolphe with a cargo of onions from Roscoff in Britanny while coming up the river to Cardigan Quay struck one of the sandbanks and opened out so badly that at high tide she was practically submerged, doing considerable damage to her cargo. She is likely to become a total wreck. The*

beach from Nantyferwig to Pen yr Ergyd is now strewn with onions.
CTA 27th August 1909
Sale of ketch. *The hull of the Dutch ketch Adolphe which stranded on the sandbanks of the Teifi was offered for sale on Thursday by Mr John Evans. The whole realised £40 12s 6d, the hulk £12*
CTA 3rd September 1909

Eos

Date wrecked 23rd June 1913
Type of vessel Fishing boat, 2 tons
Port of registry Cardigan
Eos was owned by a local fisherman and merchant seaman David Jones of Feidrfawr and used for seine netting. This is a type of fishing using a net two hundred yards or so long and weighted at the base. A rope is attached to both ends of the net. One end is held by a crewman on shore, whilst the boat is rowed in an arc, the net being paid out over it's stern. Once the boat reaches the shore the net is hauled in, hopefully along with a catch of salmon or sea trout, by pulling on the ropes at each end simultaneously. *Eos* was in the process of making her sweep and heading back for the shore when tragedy struck. The area off of Cardigan Bar where they had chosen to fish was regarded as the most dangerous part of the estuary, an area of relatively shallow ground with two distinct currents. It seems that a ground sea broke under the stern, forcing the bows under the water, catapulting the fishermen into the water. All the crew were able to swim, but sadly all were also wearing heavy clothing. Three of the crew clung to the upturned hull whilst one man struck out for the shore. Their plight was instantly recognised and two boats were launched from opposite sides of the river to attempt a rescue. Only the boat launched from the Pembrokeshire side could reach the stricken boat. By the time the rescuers arrived only one man, Washington Thomas, was left. The inquest arrived at a verdict of accidental death by drowning on the three fishermen.

Clara

Date wrecked 18th March 1915
Official no. 86524
Built Plymouth, 1884
Type of vessel Ketch, 33 tons
Port of registry Milford Haven
Lifeboat services in the bay. *On Thursday morning between eight and nine the ketch Clara, from Milford, which arrived in the bay the night before with a cargo of coal for Mr T Ll Williams, the Factory, St Dogmaels was observed to be flying signals of distress. The life-boat crew were immediately summoned and in a very short time proceeded to the vessel and took the crew of two men off. There was a strong wind blowing accompanied with heavy falls of snow. The ketch later in the day dragged her anchors and stranded on the beach and is now likely to become a total wreck. There was a high sea on at the time, described by some as the heaviest seen*

in the bay for some years past.
CTA 19th March 1915

Herefordshire
Date wrecked 15th March 1934
Official no. 120903
Built Belfast, 1905
Type of vessel. Steamer, 7217 grt
Port of Registry Liverpool

At 452 feet long *SS Herefordshire* is the largest vessel to have been wrecked on the coast of Ceredigion. Built for the Bibby Steamship Company Limited of 26 Chapel Street, Liverpool, SS *Herefordshire* had been built in 1905 by Harland and Wolff. She had spent the best part of her thirty years trading between Britain and ports in India, Burma and Sri Lanka. Her working life at an end, her pink and black painted funnel now weather beaten and tarnished, she had been laid up at Dartmouth. Now recently sold to a firm of ship-breakers and fortunately insured for £10,000, it was to the Clyde that she was being towed by two tugs when the first towrope broke off Strumble Head at about 2.30pm. The remaining tug continued to defy the elements until the second towrope broke at 3.13am. The Fishguard lifeboat was called out but was unable to take off the four men aboard the *SS Herefordshire*. By now the *SS Herefordshire* was being propelled sideways by a south westerly gale and went ashore at the north-west end of Cardigan Island. At first the four crewmen (Robert MacKenzie, John Walker, John Arthur and Robert Bird, all of Glasgow) were undecided as to what to do. However, after twenty minutes of being battered against the rocks, *SS Herefordshire* was riddled with holes and in imminent danger of breaking up. The crewmen had no option but to scramble ashore and scale the 150 foot cliffs of Cardigan Island. This they achieved safely and were soon spotted. Their escape from the island was completed using a breeches buoy. Unfortunately, it was not just the four seamen that clambered onto Cardigan Island. Sensing disaster the rats in her hold abandoned ship and, over the next few years, decimated the Puffin population. It was not until some sixty years later that nesting Puffins were to return to Cardigan Island after the descendants of the rats had been eradicated. As *Herefordshire* took some time to sink below the waves she became a profitable sideline for local boatmen running trips for visitors to see the wreck.

Below, a postcard posted aboard SS *Herefordshire* in 1908 when she was at the height of her career, many years before her one and only visit to Cardigan Island.

CHAPTER 2

Aberporth, Tresaith, Llangrannog & New Quay

Until motorised transport became the norm in Britain, bulky goods such as coal, fertiliser, limestone and building materials continued to be brought to remote coastal communities such as Tresaith, Llangrannog and Aberporth by sailing vessels. None of these small villages had any harbour facilities, and all are exposed to the prevailing south-westerly winds. By necessity these vessels needed to be small, usually ketches of no more than fifty tons. Vessels would run up onto the beach at high tide, unload their cargo into a succession of small carts as the tide receded and, hopefully, be on their way on the next incoming tide. It is not difficult to understand what could very easily go wrong should an unexpected wind blow from the south-west. Perhaps the most surprising fact is how few of these vessels were caught out and wrecked - an indication of the skills of the crews and captains.

New Quay is the one settlement covered in this chapter that possesses a purpose-built harbour. A report published in 1833 on the need for a better harbour at New Quay lists the wrecks of *Mary Fell*, *Eclipse* and *Venerable*, along with narrow escapes to the *Helen* in 1814, *Royal George* and *Nelly* in 1832. New Quay was also renowned as having been a haunt of smugglers and possibly even wreckers. When Howell Harris, the religious reformer, visited the area he condemned the inhabitants for their inhuman treatment of shipwrecked mariners, also their habit of plundering wrecks and cheating the King of his excise duties. It was suggested that mariners unfortunate enough to land on the mid-Cardiganshire coast would rather fall amongst the heathen than amongst the Cardis of New Quay. Certainly the sea was seen as a source of bounty from the treatment meted out to the *Elizabeth* at Aberporth in 1816 and the *Eclipse* at New Quay three weeks later. The presence of a cluster of wrecks in the area during December 1816 and January 1817 certainly poses the question as to whether any of these vessels were deliberately lured on to this part of the coast, particularly as the inhabitants evidently imbibed to excess on the cargo of the *Elizabeth*. It may be significant that the only proven incident involving the deliberate luring of a vessel to destruction on to the coast took place in Wales, in 1773 at Anglesey suggesting that such practices did occur.

Nearly every decade witnesses at least one storm of such fury as to cause widespread destruction. That of February 1833 accounts for the loss of at least four vessels locally and was long remembered by those who witnessed it. Out of all those mentioned in this book, the most destructive and ferocious occurred on the night of 25th / 26th October 1859. The storm is best known for the loss of the *Royal Charter* with the loss of nearly five hundred lives on the coast of Anglesey. Around the coast of Britain as a whole, 133 ships were sunk, a further 90 badly damaged, and over 800 lives lost. Although the hurricane was moving in a northerly direction, with winds blowing clockwise around an eerily still centre, it was the north-westerly winds that were to do the damage along the coast of Wales. The full force of the storm was felt at New Quay, the bay wide open to the hundred-mile-an-hour gusts. The *Robust* went ashore at Pwll Morgan, whilst *Margaret* and *Mary Anne* adorned the foreshore at Traethgwyn. *Catherine*, *Hope*, *Major Nanney*, *Ellen* and *Jane Morgan* were all sunk, though the latter three were later salvaged. (This was not the first time for the demise of the *Major Nanney* to be reported as she also sank in New

Quay harbour in March 1855.) Slightly more fortunate were the schooners *Mary Hughes*, *Perseverance*, *Pearl*, *Louisa Jane* and the smacks *Gomer* and *Mary*, all listed as very badly damaged. The 76-ton schooner *Ann & Margaret* & the 291- ton barque *Syren* were both new vessels nearing completion. The force of the storm wrenched both ships from their moorings though neither came to much harm. *Syren* was blown onto the sandy beach nearby. If the storm hadn't woken the inhabitants of a cottage on the shore, then the arrival of the jib boom of *Syren* through their roof undoubtedly did. *Ann & Margaret* was finally registered in November 1859 after being repaired. To render the storm's work complete, ten fishing boats broke their moorings and were dashed to pieces. The breakwater was also severely damaged and the lighthouse on the end washed away. What is remarkable is that only one life was lost at New Quay, that of a crewman aboard the *Major Nanney*.

Later wreckage from the *Ann & Eliza* would float ashore at Aberporth. Aberystwyth escaped relatively unscathed from the storm with two vessels entering the harbour for shelter. Two un-named vessels were run ashore on the beach between Borth and Aberdyfi.

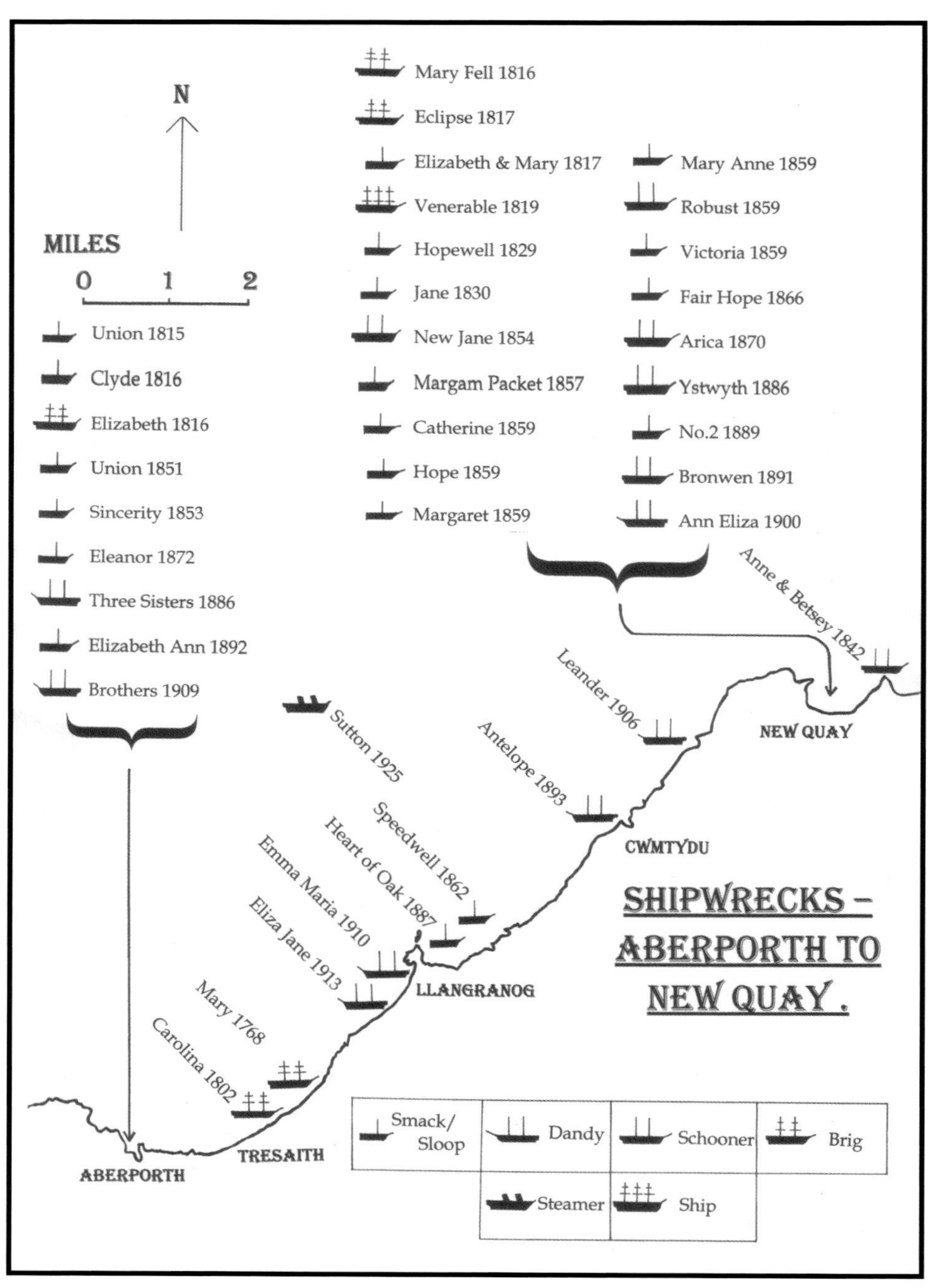
N
MILES
0 1 2
Union 1815
Clyde 1816
Elizabeth 1816
Union 1851
Sincerity 1853
Eleanor 1872
Three Sisters 1886
Elizabeth Ann 1892
Brothers 1909
Mary Fell 1816
Eclipse 1817
Elizabeth & Mary 1817
Venerable 1819
Hopewell 1829
Jane 1830
New Jane 1854
Margam Packet 1857
Catherine 1859
Hope 1859
Margaret 1859
Mary Anne 1859
Robust 1859
Victoria 1859
Fair Hope 1866
Arica 1870
Ystwyth 1886
No.2 1889
Bronwen 1891
Ann Eliza 1900
Anne & Betsey 1842
NEW QUAY
Leander 1906
Antelope 1893
CWMTYDU
Sutton 1925
Speedwell 1862
Heart of Oak 1887
Emma Maria 1910
Eliza Jane 1913
LLANGRANOG
Mary 1768
Carolina 1802
TRESAITH
ABERPORTH
SHIPWRECKS – ABERPORTH TO NEW QUAY.
Smack/ Sloop
Dandy
Schooner
Brig
Steamer
Ship

Mary
Date wrecked November 1768
Type of vessel Brig
Port of Registry Chester
Details of most shipwrecks from this period are scant and, frequently, contradictory. Although there are a number of inaccuracies in the evidence remaining, the last days of Captain Dey and the crew of the *Mary* can be pieced together. Lloyds List of Tuesday 15th November 1768 reports the loss of the *Mary*, Captain Dey, at Trackfaith, about ten miles from Cardigan. The vessel was reported to be on a voyage from Chester to London. Trackfaith could be an inaccurate spelling of either Trefdraeth (Newport) in north Pembrokeshire or Traeth Saeth, the then name for Tresaith. Both villages are approximately ten miles from Cardigan. Further evidence points to the latter. The Cardiganshire Gaol Files for the six months to April 1769 include four inquests held at Tavernseawen (probably Tafarn Siwan), Llangrannog and dealt with the deaths of Mark Dey, John Rider, Robert Wilson and an unknown male, all described as mariners of Chester. The men had been aboard a brig (erroneously referred to as *Molly* of Chester), but when near Aberporth encountered "stormy tempestuous weather and fell into the water where they suffocated and drowned." Cheshire Records Office holds a volume titled "Register of Vessels entering and leaving the Port of Chester 1740-1769". This reveals that on October 22nd 1768 *Mary* sailed from Chester with a cargo of 75 tons of cheese for London. This should have been a routine voyage for Captain Dey, as the same source showed *Mary* to have undertaken this voyage four times in the preceding two years. Deteriorating weather conditions caught out *Mary* and she foundered with the loss of four of her crew.

Carolina
Date wrecked 10th December 1802
Built Netherlands, 1797
Type of vessel Brig, 123 tons
Port of Registry Arundel
Lloyds List for Dec 14th 1802 states that "*Caroline* (sic), Capt Winter is lost on the coast of Wales, part of cargo saved" Lurking in the Cardigan Gaol Files is a document relating to a court case against a Cardigan merchant David Davies. The prosecution described Davies as "being a person of an envious, evil and wicked mind and of a most malicious disposition." He was accused of trying "to injure, oppress, aggrieve and villify the good name, fame, credit and reputation of one Harry Winter, Mariner and Thomas Davies, Merchant." This he attempted to do by writing a letter to Lloyds Coffee House, London, under the name of William John. It was from Lloyds Coffee House that matters pertaining to ship insurance were usually administered. The letter - at times rambling - is printed below. It is not entirely clear from the

documentation whether the second portion of the letter was a post scriptum to the original letter or a seperate letter written at a later date.

To the Master of Lloyds Coffee House, London

14th December 1802

Sir,
Please to inform the underwriters that the brig Caroline, Capt Winter of Arundel bound from Dublin to London with beef and butter stranded at Traethsaith on the 10th inst and wrecked all to pieces on the creek that night & c. It is thought by most seafaring men that she did not come fairly by her death and by all that can be learned that said vessel might reach Fishguard if not Milford with less ease than she could be brought to Traethsaith for [Carolina] *was seen hovering at sea all day on the 10th and never attempted to bear down towards Milford tho' the wind was favourable to that quarter. A great call* [deal?] *of the butter came up but very few casks of beef, if any was put in. The vessel call[ed] on the 10th in the morning at Aberporth and was directed to keep out to sea and bear downwards to Milford which the inhabitants thought and if she could go upwards she might reach Stadwells* [St Tudwals?] *and have not the less doubt if proper inquiry will be made but something will transpire from the crew that will enlighten the eyes of many in this transaction. Capt Pritchard of this town came out of Dublin the same tide and he made Milford, also Capt Griffith Morgan of this town was coming here and he made Cardigan Bay and if you want to know the address to write to proper persons to make some enquiry concerning the said business I recommend to you to Mr Evan Davies, Attorney at Law and Mr David Davies merchant both of Cardigan, men of honour and veracity.*

I am sir your most humble servant,

William John, master of a small sloop, Cardigan.

[PS] Capt Winter has ingratiated himself into the favour of Mr Thos. Davies merchant in Cardigan who pretend to be a kind of an agent for the underwriters that go hand in hand for a Prog [profit?] *there is auction to be tomorrow of the mast, yards and co. and the damage*[d] *butter is brought to Cardigan mostly. The pretended agent has made some good pickings from the Acton and other stranded vessels under pretence to do good to the underwriters. Auction should be as public as possible and not to keep it private in order that pretended agent might purchase the whole at half value and if this business will be left unnoticed make no doubt that the Welsh people will know the way to get new vessels for old ones.*

Despite pleading 'not guilty', David Davies was found guilty of libel and sentenced to six months imprisonment and fined £100. It may be that Davies' greatest crime may have been to publicise the nefarious business practices in the Cardigan area relating to shipwrecks.
Despite the assertion in Lloyds List, and the above letter, as to the destruction of the *Carolina*, she was still sailing under the command of Captain Henry Winter in 1805.

Unity
Date wrecked 9th March 1807
Type of vessel Sloop, 80 tons
Port of Registry Wexford
During a heavy gale this sloop was seen to go on shore between New Quay and Aberaeron. Such was the ferocity of the storm that the vessel was reduced to matchwood. Although parts of her sails and rigging were recovered, no clue as to her identity could be found, other than an oar marked 'W.P. & Co.' Neither were there any signs of the crew, giving rise to the belief that all hands had perished. Her cargo of coal was liberally strewn across the beach. All was not as it seemed. The vessel was the *Unity*, carrying a cargo of coal from Liverpool to Waterford. In Cardigan Bay she had sprung a leak and as the water gained on the vessel the master, Jasper English, had ordered the crew into the ships boat. They were picked up shortly afterwards by a smuggling vessel and landed safely at New Quay the day after the vessel had so spectacularly gone to pieces.

Unknown fishing boat
Date wrecked 16th November 1815
Type of vessel Smack
The high price of herring is emphasised by this sad incident recorded in the Cardigan Gaol Files for 1815, which includes an inquest into the death of John Davies from the parish of Penbryn, and six other fishermen who drowned when their fishing boat sank near Aberporth. Fishermen were particularly vulnerable when their boats capsized, as not only did many not swim, but they could also become tangled in their own nets.

Clyde
Date wrecked 18th Nov 1816
Type of vessel Sloop
Port of registry Saltcoats, Ayrshire
The sloop Clyde, Duncan, of Saltcoats drove on shore at Aberporth.
The Cambrian 22/11/1816

Mary Fell
Date wrecked 12th November 1816
Built Workington, 1813
Type of vessel Brig, 153 tons
Port of registry Workington
Mary Fell marked the start of a bonanza for the inhabitants of New Quay as three more ships were to be wrecked in the vicinity in as many weeks. Sailing from Liverpool to Buenos Aires she came ashore on Llanina beach with what were

described as bale goods, i.e. a general cargo packed in bales of canvas or other material and secured with ropes. *Mary Fell* was eventually dragged off Llanina beach on the second attempt and successfully salvaged. The owners of her cargo, it seems, lost patience as the crockery aboard *Mary Fell* was offered for sale locally in late January 1817.

Elizabeth

Date wrecked 13th December 1816
Type of vessel Brig
Port of registry French
The *Elizabeth* was a French vessel reported as sailing from Cette to Le Havre under the command of Captain Andre. Even by the standards of the day, Captain Andre's navigation skills must be under suspicion. The crew and part of the cargo were reported as being saved. At the time the incident was regarded as a deliberate wrecking instigated by the inhabitants of Aberporth. *Elizabeth* was carrying a cargo of wine that soon fell into the hands of the local populace, ensuring the prospect of a merry Christmas for all in the vicinity. John Jenkins, one of those involved, "died owing to intoxication cold & suffocation, found dead on beach in parish of Penbryn where a foreign vessel loaded with wine was wrecked & drank to excess the said wine." Another victim of his own excess was William Jones, "who drank too much and fell over a rock of great height into a stream of water & was carried by the flood." One source records that there were seven deaths as a result of over indulgence, though there is no evidence for this in the Cardigan Gaol Files. Others would have perished had it not been for the intervention of a local doctor. Some regarded these untimely deaths as divine retribution.

As a result of this incident, no lesser person than the Bishop of St Davids took an interest. He wrote to the clergy "whose parishes lie on the sea coast that they will lose no time in representing to their congregations in terms 'sharper than a two edged sword' the cruel and unchristian like enormity of plundering wrecks and that for the future they will preach to them on the subject once a quarter the flagrant criminality of this inhuman practice."

The wine that was salvaged was sold by auction at Cardigan on 9th September 1818. The wine consisted of ten casks of 'Bordelaises vin de Montagne', twenty five casks of 'Muid de Vin Rouge' and one cask of 'Vin Blanc'.

Eclipse

Date wrecked 6th January 1817
Type of vessel Brig
The fate of the American brig *Eclipse,* wrecked at New Quay on 6th January 1817, and the third vessel to be wrecked there within the space of a few weeks, is best followed through the newspaper articles of the day. The fate of other vessels wrecked in the vicinity

can be surmised by the treatment meted out to the wreck by the local population

The Eclipse, Qualtrough from Liverpool to Rio Janeiro was at anchor near Cardigan Bay on Friday in distress having lost her rudder on a sandbank to the northward of Tuskar Rock. It is supposed that she went off to the northward as she was not seen on Saturday when it blew a very heavy gale from the southwest
Lloyds List, January 10th 1817

Eclipse, Qualtrough, from Liverpool to Rio Janeiro put into New Quay Bay near Cardigan 5th inst; the next day she drove across the Mary Fell master Wallis from Liverpool to Buenos Aires and afterwards grounded and sunk in about two fathoms, at low water. The Mary Fell was driven on shore on a sandy beach, the same night but had not received any apparent damage.
The Cambrian 17th January 1817

We are sorry to record the destruction of another vessel on the coast of Cardigan viz the Eclipse, of Liverpool, bound for Buenos Aires with a valuable general cargo which was stranded a few evenings since in New Quay Bay and became a total wreck; the crew were fortunately saved by the fishermen, after enduring the greatest hardships having clung to the mast all night. Col Jones of Llanina, with the most laudible promptitude swore in a number of special constables to protect such part of the cargo as came on shore but all their exertions could not prevent the partial plunder of the country people, according to their usual inhuman custom. The cargo was insured for £52000. Col Jones activity on this occasion is conjectured to have exposed him to the diabolical revenge of some of the disappointed wreckers; his house having been forcibly entered by four fellows habited like seamen, on the night of the 20th ult. The barking of a dog alarmed the butler, who, armed with a brace of pistols, encountered the robbers in a passage leading from the back kitchen and discharged one of his pistols at them, but it is supposed, without effect; the other unluckily missed fire and the villains made a precipitate retreat. Col Jones speedily came armed with a loaded gun to the assistance of his courageous and faithful butler, but the nocturnal depredators had completely disappeared.
The Cambrian 1st February 1817

Elizabeth & Mary
Date wrecked 18th January 1817
Built Stockton on Tees
Type of vessel Sloop, 63 tons
Port of registry Liverpool
Having arrived to retrieve some of the cargo of the *Mary Fell* for return to Liverpool, *Elizabeth & Mary* "drove on some rocks in Cardigan Bay 18th instant and it is supposed would be totally lost"
The Cambrian 3rd January1817

Venerable
Date wrecked 18th January 1819
Built 1799
Type of vessel Ship, 275 tons
Port of Registry Liverpool
Captained by Capt A Elliott, *Venerable* was returning from the coast of Africa to Liverpool. Her cargo included ivory and palm oil and was valued at £25,000. Since leaving Africa fifteen weeks earlier, she had not sighted land until she saw Strumble Head. On Monday the 18th of January 1819 she was driven into New Quay Bay, running on shore about five o'clock in the evening and quickly became a total wreck. The crew, 18 in number, were all saved as (it was hoped) would be the greater part of the cargo. Three active local magistrates of the county, J W Lewis, A T Gwynne and J J Jones esqrs, were much praised in the newspaper account of the wreck for their unwearied and successful exertions in protecting the cargo from "the plunder by the inhuman wretches who infest the coast". All of these gentlemen remained on the beach during the whole of the first night to protect the vessel.

Hopewell
Date wrecked August 1829
Built Craig-las beach, 1810
Type of vessel Sloop, 27 tons
Port of registry Cardigan
Built nineteen years earlier at Craig-las, Llanrhystud, *Hopewell* was typical of the vessels sailing in Cardigan Bay at this time, being 13ft 4ins long and 6ft 4ins wide. Owned by the Phillips family, she was lost at New Quay in August 1829.

Jane
Date wrecked 24th Nov 1830
Built Aberporth, 1787
Type of vessel Sloop 29 tons
Port of registry Aberystwyth
Jane was lost off New Quay Head. Her certificate of registry was delivered up and cancelled on the 16th Aril 1831. The fact that her ships papers were saved suggests that the crew were able to evacuate her in an orderly fashion.

Anne & Betsey
Date wrecked 26th January 1842
Built Aberystwyth 1807
Type of vessel Sloop
Port of registry Aberystwyth
Anne & Betsey, Thomas Delahoyde master, broke from her moorings during a storm and went on shore near Llanina. She was dashed to pieces shortly afterwards. Lloyds List noted that as a result of the storm, regarded by some as a hurricane, "Many ships are supposed to have foundered as the coast appears strewed with masts and spars"

Mary & Anne
Date wrecked 26th January 1842
A victim of the same storm a similar fate befell *Mary & Anne*, Captain Watkins, as the above mentioned *Anne & Betsey*. Again, it seems that she broke free from her moorings, went on shore and was dashed to pieces shortly afterwards.

Union

Date wrecked 5th September 1851
Type of vessel Sloop, 20 tons
Port of registry Cardigan
Lost near Aberporth in unknown circumstances.

Sincerity

Date wrecked 18th December 1853
Built Aberdyfi, 1803
Type of vessel Smack, 45 tons
Port of registry Aberystwyth
Aberystwyth - The Late Gales – Loss of a ship. The Sincerity, David Jenkins master, has been wrecked off Aberporth, about eight miles below New Quay. She sailed from Milford at half past five pm on Saturday the 17th instant bound from Bristol to this town, the wind at the time being SSE and was off Cemaes Head, Cardigan Bay at two a.m. on Sunday morning being about ten miles off New Quay Head. It blew a whole gale of wind from S.E. with sudden squalls. The crew weighed the ship round to endeavour to try and get her under hand, but the foresail was split as was also the double reef mainsail. They then endeavoured to get her into Llangrannog Bay but failed and ran for Aberporth without sails to try and save the ship and cargo when she struck upon a reef of rocks and was totally wrecked by the ground sea on Sunday night and most of the general cargo was lost, but all lives were saved in a boat by the assistance of eighteen men from Aberporth. The vessel was insured in the Mutual Ship Insurance society of this town, but the cargo was not with only one exception. The losses will be considerable varying from £50 to £250. The Bee, Edward Hall master, sailed from Milford the same day as the Sincerity bound for Aberystwyth but she could not keep the land and was driven to Wicklow, having lost her boat and all other materials on deck.
The Welshman, 23rd December 1853

However old habits die hard. The report of the same incident in the *Carnarvon & Denbigh Herald* puts a slightly different gloss on the proceedings. "The people of Aberporth behaved shamefully on the occasion, though called out from chapel to render assistance, which they did so far as the lives of the master and crew were concerned, but they plundered the goods in all directions and ended the affair by rioting and becoming thoroughly drunk, having opened a pipe of wine and other vessels containing liquor."
The goods being carried in the *Sincerity* were for a number of Aberystwyth shopkeepers In total the cargo was valued at £1500. Only one consignment, worth £150 for Mr Richard Roberts the druggist, was insured.

New Jane

Date wrecked 20th December 1854
Type of vessel Schooner, 110 tons
Port of registry Exeter
New Jane became stranded and eventually broke up at the back of the

Pier Head at New Quay in a force ten storm blowing from the northwest. The loss was in part due to the master not knowing this part of the coast well. The vessel was insured for £500 and the cargo of coal a further £65.

Margam Packet
Date wrecked 13th March 1857
*Official no.*18975
Built Bristol, 1828
Type of vessel Sloop, 30 tons
Port of registry Swansea
This aging vessel arrived at New Quay in a leaky state carrying a cargo of timber from Milford Haven. The available records suggest that she expired rather than sank and, being beyond economical repair, was broken up.

Robust
Official no. 15708
Date wrecked 25th October 1859
Built Miramichi, 1837
Type of vessel Schooner, 76tons
Port of registry Aberystwyth
Failing to live up to her name, *Robust* became a victim of the *Royal Charter* gale. This vessel, master Thomas Williams, was wrecked at Pwll Morgan beach, New Quay. She had previously hoped to ride out the storm at Porthor Bay, near Pwllheli en route to Liverpool but had parted from her anchor and chain. She was then forced to run before the wind. The crew attempted to save the vessel by throwing the deck cargo of timber overboard but their attempts in the teeth of a hurricane proved fruitless, however, they managed to save themselves.

Victoria
Date wrecked 25th October 1859
Official no. 10661
Built Aberystwyth, 1845
Type of vessel Sloop, 31 tons
Port of registry Aberystwyth
Sailing to Weston super Mare with a cargo of Porthmadog slates, Captain Enos encountered the full fury of the *Royal Charter* gale. Propelled from behind by hurricane force winds, *Victoria* was forced to run into New Quay seeking shelter. She was totally wrecked at Cei Bach but all the crew were saved. Parts of the rigging, sails, chains and cables were salvaged from the wreck.

Margaret
Date wrecked 25th October 1859
Type of vessel Sloop
Port of registry Cardigan
Parted her moorings at the height of the gale and went to pieces on Traethgwyn.

Mary Anne
Date wrecked 25th October 1859
Another vessel that parted her moorings and drifted onto Traethgwyn beach where she was wrecked.

Catherine
Date wrecked 25th October 1859

Hope

Date wrecked 25th October 1859

These two vessels, captained by Messrs Davies and Thomas, respectively, were both wrecked at New Quay, exact circumstances unknown.

Eliza & Jane

Date wrecked 26th Oct 1859

Port of Registry Porthmadog

Following the storms the night before, wreckage (evidently from a Porthmadog vessel) drifted ashore at Aberporth. Initially, identification could not be made as only a letter 'A' could be deciphered. Subsequently more wreckage which identified the vessel as the *Eliza & Jane* was brought into Cardigan.

Speedwell

Date wrecked 2nd September 1862

*Official no.*10273

Built Llangrannog, 1822

Type of vessel Sloop, 26 tons

Port of registry Cardigan

The Speedwell (smack) of Cardigan ran on shore last night at Llangrannog and became a total wreck. Two men drowned.

LL 06/09/1862

Fair Hope

Date wrecked 27th February 1866

Official no. 9840

Built Aberaeron, 1838

Type of vessel Sloop, 37 tons

Port of Registry Aberystwyth

Vessel wrecked at New Quay, circumstances unknown.

Arica

Date wrecked 22nd November 1870

Official no. 21752

Built Aberaeron, 1858

Type of vessel Schooner, 111 tons

Port of registry Aberystwyth

Despite there being three newspapers carrying news from the New Quay area, the fate of *Arica* received scant attention locally. Her demise received most attention in the *Shipping & Mercantile Gazette.*

Aberaeron Nov 22nd WNW, heavy gale, thick rain. The schooner Arica, Rees, of this port from Waterford went on shore on New Quay head having become unmanageable due to a heavy squall; crew saved but the vessel will become a total wreck.

SMG 24th November1870

The crew were able to save themselves by scrambling on to the rocks on which the vessel was grounded. *Arica* was dashed to pieces shortly afterwards.

Eleanor

Date wrecked 15th October 1872

Official no. 16142

Type of vessel Fishing boat, 8 tons

Port of registry Cardigan

At 3pm on a Tuesday afternoon the 8-ton fishing boat *Eleanor* containing a crew of seven left St Dogmaels for the herring fishery grounds. The weather was described as thick and raining. The fishing grounds were reached and the nets shot about 5.30pm. Two hours later the nets were hauled in and the boat started back. Due to the high wind that had got up *Eleanor* anchored under Pencribach point slightly to the north west of Aberporth and remained there until 10pm. At this time the wind was coming from the north-northwest. As the wind was increasing in strength the crew decided to head for Aberporth under the mainsail with the peak dropped. About four hundred yards from shore the boat broached and shortly afterwards capsized when a wave broke on the port side. Two men clung to the vessel for an hour then swam in. All the others are believed to have been washed out to sea. Had they remained where they were, under Pencribach, all would have been saved. The drowned men were T Rees, John Morgans, Thomas Lewis, J Llywellyn and Thomas Davies. One of the survivors cut away his trousers and boots as soon as he landed in the water and this is thought to have saved him.

Three Sisters

Date wrecked 17th October 1886
Built Ceibach, 1882
Type of vessel Ketch, 36 tons
Port of Registry Cardigan
Wrecked "at the furthest extremity of the beach" at Aberporth in company of another un-named fishing boat on 17th October 1886.

Ystwyth

Date wrecked 8th December 1886
Official no. 42580
Built Aberystwyth, 1861
Type of vessel Schooner, 61 tons
Port of Registry Aberystwyth
Invariably, newspaper accounts are not always accurate. This is exemplified by the case of the Aberystwyth schooner *Ystwyth* in 1886. Carrying a cargo of coal from Porthcawl to Aberystwyth, *Ystwyth* encountered a severe storm (the same storm that washed away Trefechan Bridge in Aberystwyth) and went for shelter in New Quay. Both the Aberystwyth Observer and the Cambrian News reported that she had broken free from her moorings and sank becoming a total wreck. Neither the vessel nor her cargo of coal were insured. Other records, however, give a different story. Encountering heavy weather on 6th Dec 1886 *Ystwyth* did indeed put into New Quay. Having broken free from her moorings two days later, it seems considerable damage was done. In true Cardiganshire fashion (and to prevent unnecessary expenditure) the crew were immediately discharged. However her owner, David Thomas, of Great Darkgate Street, Aberystwyth, had enough faith in *Ystwyth* to repair her. *Ystwyth* continued to sail the coastal waters of the western seaboard until 1891. Her 1887 crew agreements states "Jan 1887-Jul 1887. No voyages have been made nor any crew engaged during the above dates the within named vessel having sunk in New Quay harbour during the gale of the 8th day of December 1886 where she

remained in repairing etc till Aug 8th 1887 when she was brought to Aberystwyth to be completed and is now loading a cargo of pitwood for Porthcawl."

No2

Date wrecked 9th October 1889
Type of vessel Pilot cutter, 10 tons
Port of registry Wexford
NEW QUAY. Shipwreck. *During the last severe gales pilot boat No2 of the Wexford Harbour commissioners broke adrift from her moorings in Wexford Haven and drifted out to sea. Early on the morning of 9th October the boat was discovered on the beach at Traethgwyn. At the time she was in good condition with both masts standing though full of water. As the tide ebbed however the boat began to break up and in a short time the masts went by the board and the shore was strewn with wreckage. The bottom was washed clean off with the ballast – castings and pig iron upon it. The coastguards took charge of the wreck and the materials, timber, canvas, ropes etc were conveyed into the adjacent field beyond the reach of the waves where they now remain pending the usual sale on such occasions. It is extraordinary that such a vessel could be blown across the channel without having been observed and boarded.*
CN 18th October 1889

Bronwen

Date wrecked 21st September 1891
Official no. 98928
Built Ardrossan, 1891
Type of vessel Schooner, 99 tons
Port of registry London
On Monday afternoon a vessel was spotted coming into New Quay Bay. Observers noticed that she seemed to be struggling and only just responded sufficiently to the helm to clear Carreg Gwalltog. The captain saw no hope of clearing the next point and dropped anchor. In a few minutes, at about six p.m. she struck within a few yards of the spot where the *Arica* was lost twenty years before. The rocket brigade was soon on shore opposite the *Bronwen*, having dragged and carried the necessary apparatus over rocks and boulders to the scene of the disaster. The rocket however was not needed as the vessel was only drawing five feet of water and washed so close to the shore that the crew, by attaching a rope to a lifebuoy, were able to communicate with the shore from the foremast. The rocket brigade worked hard in effecting the rescue and but for the brave manner in which the shipwrecked were met they would undoubtedly never have reached the shore. One member of the brigade, O T Owen especially distinguished himself being washed off his feet several times in the course of rescuing the crew of *Bronwen*. In a very short time the brigade, ropes attached to their bodies assisting the crew through the strong backwash. First off the *Bronwen* was a native of Ballyshannon followed by the Norwegian mate who fastened to his body a bag containing his clothes; the

third to take to the rope was the ship's sixteen year old boy, William Parkin of Glasgow. The only effects he brought with him were his bible and a picture of his mother. The fourth off was a native of Dublin, the fifth Captain Mendus. The crew were taken care of by the local agent of the Shipwrecked Mariners society and comfortably lodged at London House.

By 8 p.m. the same evening *Bronwen*'s foremast had gone. The nature of the ground, rocky and boulders, ensured that she couldn't be got off. By Tuesday she had become a complete wreck.

Bronwen shortly before her demise at New Quay, 1891.
(courtesy Amgueddfa Ceredigion)

Three artefacts salvaged from *Bronwen*, the wheel boss, a letter opener and her name board. (courtesy Amgueddfa Ceredigion)

Elizabeth Ann

Date wrecked 28th April 1892
Official no. 69852
Built Cardigan, 1875
Type of vessel Smack, 38 tons
Port of Registry Cardigan
The smack Elizabeth Ann of Aberporth (Capt T Thomas, Ddol, Aberporth master & owner) has become a total wreck. The Elizabeth Ann arrived here [at Aberporth] two or three days ago discharged her cargo and got ballasted; on Wednesday she went out about half a mile from the shore and rode at anchor in the bay, awaiting orders

which were expected by Thursday mornings post but sad to relate that morning she was in a thousand pieces. It was blowing hard the first part of Wednesday night and about midnight the wind increased to a strong gale. Soon after one of the anchor chains parted and the vessel drifted on the rocks about 3am when the cable parted. Capt Thomas realising his perilous position shot up some rockets as signals of distress which were instantly noticed by his sister and some friends ashore who immediately endeavoured to render assistance but before anyone had time to reach the spot where the ship struck the rocks the crew of three had got ashore; the first to leave the vessel was a youth of about 17 years of age, named David Thomas of Tremain; directly the ship struck and stopped on the flat rock he had lowered himself by a rope from the side of the ship down on the rock but unfortunately he must have been swept back to the sea by a wave and got drowned, as he has not been seen since. The captain and the mate got on the rocks in a little while and were sadly amazed to find the lad wasn't there. It was very fortunate that the tide was out at the time or very probably the ship would have drifted down the coast and run against some of the larger rocks that exist between Aberporth and Tresaith in which case all hands would have likely perished. We understand the vessel was insured.
CTA 29th April 1892

Antelope
Date wrecked 26th August 1893
Official no 56402
Built New Quay, 1868
Type of vessel Ketch, 29 tons
Port of registry Aberystwyth
After unloading her cargo on the beach, *Antelope* was trying to manoeuvre out of the confines of Cwmtydu in windy conditions. Things did not go according to plan and *Antelope* drifted on to the rocks. She soon became a total wreck. Her crew saved themselves, with difficulty, by climbing over the cliffs.

Ann Eliza
Date wrecked 17th November 1900
*Official no.*16113
Built Cardigan, 1855
Type of vessel Ketch, 43 tons
Port of registry Cardigan
Evan Powell Jenkins, Pentre Arms, Llangrannog purchased *Ann Eliza* in 1888 and converted her into a ketch. She was wrecked on Traethgwyn beach, New Quay after the three crew were rescued by the Cardigan lifeboat *Frank and Marion.*

Leander
Date wrecked 19th November 1906
*Official no.*27309
Built Llansantffraed, 1859
Type of vessel Ketch, 54 tons
Port of registry Caernarfon
At the time of her loss *Leander* was carrying ten tons of sand as ballast. She departed Waterford for Y Felinheli

on 18th November at high water (9am) the weather being fine and clear. All went well until ten o'clock in the evening, when a gale sprang up from the northwest with heavy seas. About ten miles southeast of Wicklow Head all sail except the standing jib was taken in, and *Leander* attempted to keep to her course.

By 2pm the next afternoon it was still blowing a gale from the north-northwest, and the vessel was four miles or so from land. The captain and crew were unable to distinguish any landmarks and were rapidly being blown on shore. A mile or so from land the captain (and owner) Richard Foulkes was able to distinguish New Quay Head. Extra canvas was put on in the hope of making New Quay harbour. This was not to be, and the extra canvas was taken off and the two anchors let go. The port chain soon parted under the strain and signals of distress were put up. The local lifeboat promptly rescued the captain and two crew. Shortly after their rescue the starboard chain parted and *Leander* drove ashore about one mile south of New Quay. As the tide receded she keeled over, the deck facing the wrath of the sea.

The Cambrian News dated 30th Nov 1906 reported that Leander was still stranded on Traethgwyn beach despite efforts to re-float her.

Elizabeth

Date wrecked 2nd October 1908
Official no. 12386
Built Trefriw, 1847
Type of vessel Ketch, 38 tons
Port of Registry Cardigan

***A vessel founders in the Bay** – On Friday morning last the ketch Elizabeth, formerly of Caernarfon, latterly of Cardigan left the latter place with a cargo of bricks from Cardigan brickworks at about 9.30 for New Quay, the wind at the time being about SE. Outside the bar the wind was blowing ENE and a tack had to be made about seven miles from land when she became becalmed. The pumps were tried and she was found to be making no water. About 4.30pm the pumps were again tried when it was found the water was gaining proving she had somehow sprung a leak and the crew consisting of Captain Williams, also the owner, and the mate Benjamin Richards had to abandon her about 9 o'clock, the water then being four or five inches over the cabin floor. The ketch probably sank around midnight five miles ENE of New Quay. The two men took to their boat and landed on Mwnt beach where they spent the night.*

CTA 9th October1908

Brothers

Date wrecked 17th November 1909
Official no. 1877
Built Cardigan, 1848
Type of vessel Ketch, 38 tons
Port of registry Cardigan

On the rocks – the smack Brothers owned by Mr Thomas, Plas` in trying to sail out of Aberporth on Wednesday

morning was blown by a strong northeasterly wind on the rocks near Dolwen. All efforts to save her have so far been unsuccessful. It is more than likely she will become a total wreck.
CTA 19th November 1909.

Originally built as a smack, *Brothers* was converted into a dandy in 1892 after nearly being wrecked.

Emma Maria
Date wrecked 19th October 1910
Official no. 67134
Built Whitehaven 1872
Type of vessel Ketch, 35 tons
Port of registry Liverpool
Lost on Llangranog beach whilst attempting to unload a cargo of basic slag (a form of fertiliser) from Liverpool. A south westerly blew up and wrecked her on Llangrannog beach.

Psychcia
Date wrecked 23rd Jan 1912
Built Dartmouth, 1898
Type of vessel Steam yacht, 20 tons.
Port of Registry Chester
Used by her owner Jenkin Thomas of 11 Park Street, New Quay, for cruising in the bay during the summer months *Psychcia* was moored securely fore and aft five hundred yards south west from New Quay Pier-head. During the evening of the 23rd January, a heavy ground sea set in and the vessel strained at her moorings. About high tide the stern chain parted and the vessel swung round with her bow pointing to the northwest. Shortly after she drove ashore broadside on and was holed by a large boulder. Emergency repairs were effected and attempts made to pull her off the beach. These were unsuccessful, and on the 2nd February, another storm drove the vessel on to rough ground where she broke up. The vessel was valued at £700 but only insured for £500.

Eliza Jane
Date wrecked 23rd Sept 1913
*Official no.*47050
Built Bangor, 1866
Type of vessel Ketch
Port of registry Beaumaris
Another ketch caught in an exposed position on Llangrannog beach whilst unloading a cargo of culm (fine coal) from Swansea. The vessel was battered against the rocks at Pentrwyn and became a total loss. She, too, was the property of E P Jenkins of Pentre Arms, Llangrannog .

Sutton
Date wrecked 27th Nov 1925
Official no. 143676
Built Selby, 1920
Type of vessel Steamship, 485 grt
Port of Registry Liverpool
Sutton was one of the small number of steamers that came to Aberystwyth to collect cargo during the 1920s. Her cargo was lead and zinc concentrate, from mines at Erwtomau and Pontrhydygroes. She was loaded with 70 tons in her No1 hold and 170 tons

in her No2 hold. As high tide approached, *Sutton* fired up her boilers and cautiously negotiated her way out of Aberystwyth harbour to sail for Antwerp. Due to the silting at the entrance to the harbour, and her near eleven foot draft, she grounded twice as she laboured over the bar and then headed southwards into the night, accompanied by a strengthening north-westerly wind. Owned by the Overton Steamship Company of Preesons Row, Liverpool *Sutton* was one of four sister ships and a relatively new vessel which cost £30,000 to build.

Aboard were Captain Terratta, his wife, teenage son, and daughter, and the crew of eight, nearly all of them from Runcorn. Captain Terratta had been master of the *Sutton* since her launch. Lights were seen in Cardigan Bay between nine-thirty and eleven pm but were assumed to be those of a trawler working in the bay. A distinct red colour to the light was attributed to the weather conditions at the time and not identified for the distress signal it was. It seems strange in this day and age that a vessel would set sail without distress flares, but this was so in the case of the *Sutton*. What was seen from the shore was in all probability the small hand-held, self-igniting flares kept in the ship's boat. These were not distinctive enough from lights ordinarily seen in the area to be recognised for what they were and thus gave no cause for concern to those who witnessed them.

The first clue to the demise of the *Sutton* was the finding of the ships boat at Traeth Gwyryddon and the corpse of a sailor nearby the next morning. The body was identified as that of William Booth, his name being tattooed on his arm. A post mortem established that he died of exposure some hours after reaching shore. The body of Mrs Terratta was recovered shortly afterwards.

At the subsequent Board of Trade inquiry, held the following May in Cardigan, retained samples of the lead and zinc concentrates were analysed. One batch was found to contain 12.02% water, the other batch 11.47%. It was concluded that this water had risen to the top of the cargo in the holds, lubricating the ore concentrate and causing it to shift when the vessel encountered rough weather. The process may have been set in train by the bumpy departure over Aberystwyth bar. The shifting cargo caused the vessel to take on a heavy and increasing list. Eventually, the crew were forced to abandon the *Sutton* and took to the ship's boat. It was probably at this point that the hand held flares were used in an attempt to summon assistance. The ship's boat must then have capsized.

The coastguards were not wholly exonerated from blame. The watchman at Llangrannog had not been deployed on the night in question. There were problems with the telephones in the area at the time, preventing effective communication. It was the opinion of the court that all

The steamer *Sutton* seen in happier times. (courtesy David Jenkins)

sea-going vessels should be equipped with rockets or shells throwing stars to be used as distress signals. Had this been the case, twelve lives would have been saved.

Sutton is estimated to have sunk at 52 13'N, 4 39'W, *i.e.* approximately 5 miles north-west of Aberporth.

HMS Whirlwind

Date wrecked 1st November 1974
Official no. F187
Built Newcastle, 1943
Type of vessel Frigate, 1710 tons

HMS *Whirlwind* had served her country as a convoy escort in the second world war. In 1953 she had been converted from a destroyer to a frigate but twenty years on she was outdated and slow. She looked set for an ignominious end as a rust streaked target ship for the Aberporth firing range. However during a storm she broke free from her moorings and probably due to the holes in her superstructure rapidly sank. Divers who have examined the wreck report that she has not sunk into the seabed and shows considerable superficial damage, though her hull is intact. HMS *Whirlwind* lies at a depth of 31 metres at 52 16 00N 004 40 00W.

CHAPTER 3

Aberaeron, Llanon & Llanrhystud to Morfa Bychan

This stretch of coast is blessed with only one harbour, that at Aberaeron. Completed in 1811 and framed by pastel coloured regency cottages, the harbour owes its origins to the vision of Alban Thomas Jones Gwynne of nearby Llyswen. Although the harbour itself possesses a sedate and tranquil ambience, the narrow entrance with it's reliance on the tide for entry deserves much respect. Perhaps it is this tricky approach and the respect that it engenders that accounts for the very few wrecks to have occurred in the vicinity of Aberaeron. One vessel that had a fortunate escape at Aberaeron was the schooner *King of the Forest* sailing from Newport to Liverpool with a cargo of iron rails. Blown ashore she was subsequently pulled off.

Although there are no other formal port facilities on this stretch of coast, there are many features of the coastline that point to past maritime activity. Not least of these are the lime-kilns to be found at intervals all along the coast of Ceredigion. Of these the most spectacular are those to the south of Llanrhystud. Now a conservation area, the kilns nestle amongst verdant summer undergrowth giving every appearance of Mayan ruins in the jungles of South America. Lime was needed in Ceredigion to increase crop yield in the acidic and infertile soils. The nearest source of lime was Pembrokeshire, too far away to contemplate transporting laboriously a cartload at a time. Consequently, limestone was imported by sea and lime kilns built at numerous suitable landing places along the coast including Morfa Bychan, Llanrhystud and Llanon. Coal dust also had to be imported to burn the limestone and turn it into slaked lime, which once it had absorbed rainwater was ready for spreading on the land. The Cardigan Gaol Files for the six month period to September 1802 contain one document relating to the trade in limestone. This is an inquest into the death of John Morris who drowned at Aberllong beach, Llanon, attempting to stop a sloop grounding on a heap of limestone.

Also at Llanon the Aberclydan Steam Brewery flourished for many years bringing with it a maritime trade importing culm and hops and exporting the finished product. Operating the local lime-kilns was also part of the companies franchise. The brewery finally went out of business ca.1880, probably because it was unable to compete with cheaper beer imported by train from the midlands.

As with the whole of the coast of Ceredigion, wreckage from disasters further afield sometimes washed up. One such instance was in October 1852 when wreckage, including the stern, from the *Mobile*, a nearly new vessel of over 1000 tons was washed up along the coast between Aberarth and Llanrhystud. *Mobile* had struck the Blackwater Bank of the coast of Ireland in hurricane force conditions and sunk with the loss of over sixty lives.

It is along this stretch of coastline that the most photographed shipwreck in Ceredigion took place. This was the *Guiding Star*, wrecked in 1926 and photographed by, amongst others, Arthur Lewis of Aberystwyth.

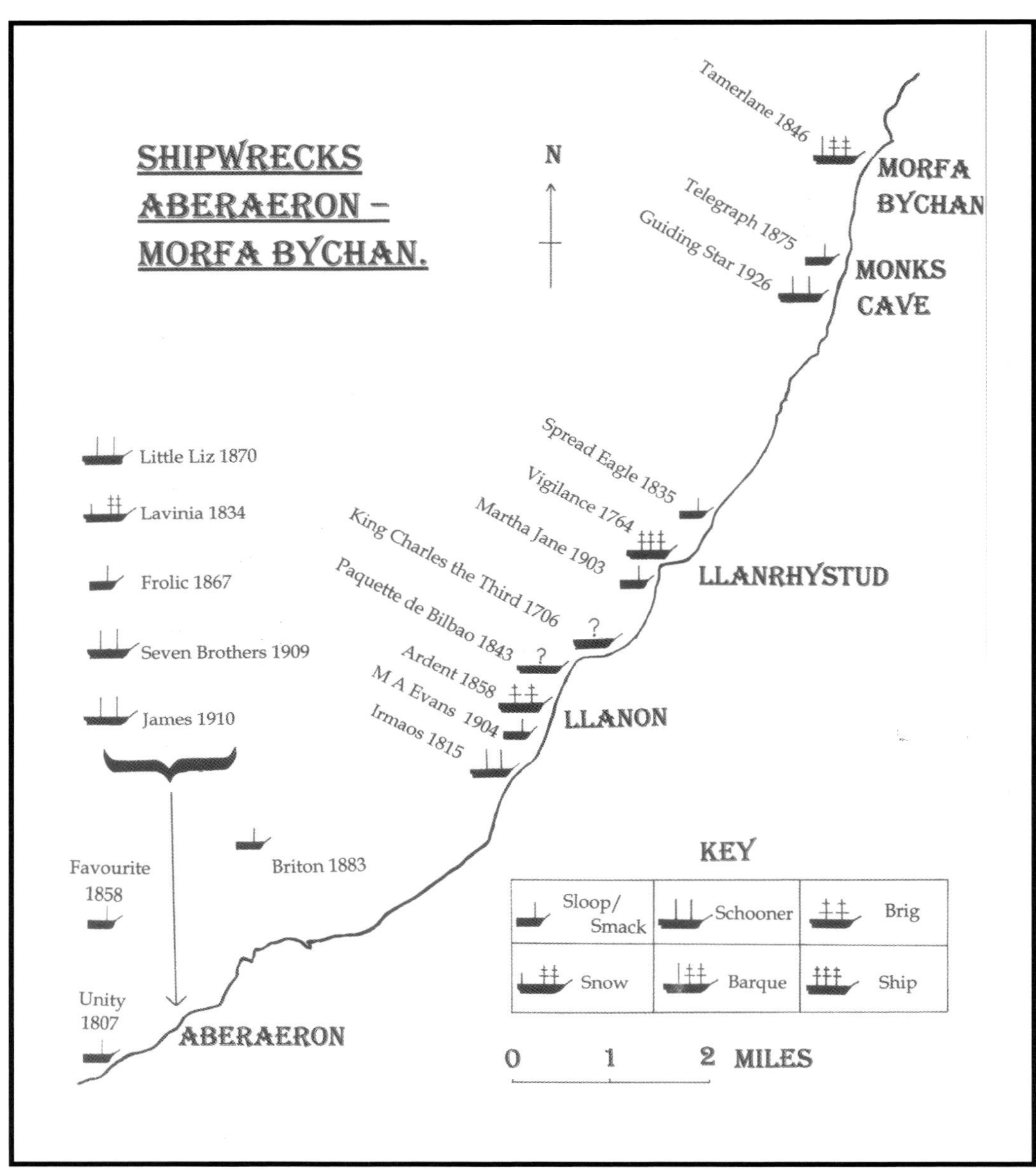

SHIPWRECKS
ABERAERON –
MORFA BYCHAN.
N
Tamerlane 1846
MORFA
BYCHAN
Telegraph 1875
Guiding Star 1926
MONKS
CAVE
Spread Eagle 1835
Vigilance 1764
Martha Jane 1903
LLANRHYSTUD
King Charles the Third 1706
?
Paquette de Bilbao 1843
?
Ardent 1858
M A Evans 1904
Irmaos 1815
LLANON
Little Liz 1870
Lavinia 1834
Frolic 1867
Seven Brothers 1909
James 1910
Favourite
1858
Briton 1883
Unity
1807
ABERAERON
KEY
Sloop/
Smack
Schooner
Brig
Snow
Barque
Ship
0
1
2
MILES

King Charles the Third

Date wrecked 6th May 1706

Carrying a cargo of 19,300 oranges and lemons and "half a ton of Portuguese wine" from Lisbon *King Charles the Third* (James Marsham, master) became stranded on the beach at Llanon. The cargo was destined for Lord Lisburne so, consequently, did not have far to travel to its final destination at Trawscoed. The port book for the Port of Cardigan records the wine was for private use. Whether the vessel was refloated or wrecked is not recorded.

Vigilance

Date wrecked February 1764

There are three sources of information that seem to refer to the wreck of the *Vigilance* near Llanrhystud. The first of these are the Tregaron Quarter Sessions for 1764. An order was made that £5 be paid to Thomas Lloyd Esquire, adjutant to the militia, in repayment of "money spent by him to the men of the Militia for their maintenance for four days in saving the goods of a ship stranded on the coast in the parish of Llanrhystud." Apart from inferring that the local militia were required to guard the wreck from the local population, the reference tells us relatively little as to the nature of the wreck. However, in the Dolaucothi correspondence in the National Library of Wales there is a letter to John Johnes from his sister, Elizabeth Lewis of Llanerchaeron, dated 12th February 1764. In the letter she talks of the wreck of a three-masted ship near Llanrhystud of about 500 tons. From the letter it is evident that the cargo included oranges and white wine. It seems that some pipes of white wine had come ashore and been "scrambled over by the country people." A pipe is a type of barrel capable of holding 105 gallons. Her letter goes on to say that the militia were employed in guarding the shore, presumably to stop any further barrels being spirited away. The writer goes on to state that she thinks that little of the wine salvaged by the local population would be recovered by the authorities. The wine was being offered for sale locally at four shillings (20p) a gallon. Elizabeth Lewis regrets not being able to procure any on behalf of her brother, but as her husband was issuing warrants against those suspected of harbouring the wine this would have been awkward. However, she goes on to say that if he is interested in obtaining supplies she "would endeavour to put him in a method to get some."

Lloyds List does not contain any reference to the loss of a ship in Cardigan Bay in early February 1764. There is however the following entry for Friday 3rd February 1764 "The *Vigilance*, Burn, from the Granadoes for Liverpool is ashore at Clugan Bay and it is feared will be lost." There is such a place as Clugan in the Orkney Islands, but no record of any shipwreck there at this time. Neither is there mention of the wreck of a vessel called *Vigiliance* anywhere else in the British Isles at this time. Bearing in mind that Lloyds List was compiled from handwritten notes sent by correspondents from all over Europe, it is not impossible that Clugan is a mis-spelling of Cardigan. *Lloyds List* has never had a good track record when dealing with Welsh place-names. If this is so, then the vessel wrecked at Llanrhystud in February 1764 was very probably *Vigilance*.

Unknown fishing boat

Date wrecked 18th November 1814
Type of vessel Fishing boat
The true cost of herring fishing is further emphasised by this sad incident recorded in the Cardigan Gaol Files for 1814, which includes inquests into the deaths of David Oliver, Lewis Davies, Thomas Davies and two Thomas Jones. All drowned when their fishing boat was overtaken by a sudden storm while attempting to enter Aberaeron Harbour. The sea was reported as running so tremendously high that, although the boat was only a stone's throw from the shore, no assistance whatever could be afforded to the unfortunate crew. *The Cambrian* newspaper recorded that of the seven men drowned, six of them were married men having no less than 27 children between them. Two other boats engaged in the same trade foundered but no lives were lost on the same night.

Irmaos

Date wrecked 11th December 1815
Built Portugal
Type of vessel Schooner, 86 tons
Port of Registry Oporto
Christmas came a fortnight early in Llanon in 1815. Father Christmas came in the guise of the Portuguese schooner *Irmaos*, which came ashore on the beach at Llanon and within half an hour was dashed to pieces. Her seasonal cargo comprised, appropriately enough, of oranges, chestnuts and corkwood.

Friendship

Date wrecked 30th March 1827
Built Cardigan
Type of vessel Sloop, 31 tons
Port of Registry Cardigan
The first inkling of the loss of the *Friendship* was the finding of part of the deck of a vessel and boat with the legend 'Friendship – Cardigan, Richard Finch' washed ashore 30th March 1827 at Llansantffraed. Several pieces of bread were also noted washed up on the beach. According to the Carmarthen Journal, the 31-ton sloop *Friendship*, Richard Finch master, was bound from Cardigan to Belfast with a cargo of slates. All the hands, three in number, perished when the vessel sank off the coast, probably somewhere between New Quay and Llanon. The presence of something as fragile as bread washed up on the shore at Llanon suggests that the vessel came to grief nearby. Despite the loss of life, the owners

were keen to salvage what they could, going to the trouble of issuing flyers in the district.

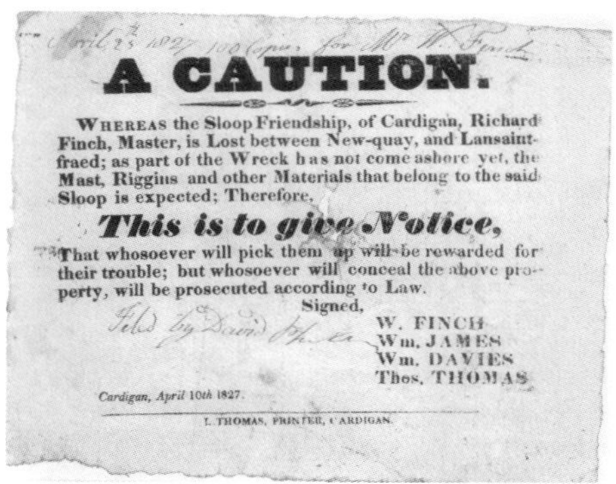

A CAUTION.

WHEREAS the Sloop Friendship, of Cardigan, Richard Finch, Master, is Lost between New-quay, and Lansaintfraed; as part of the Wreck has not come ashore yet, the Mast, Riggins and other Materials that belong to the said Sloop is expected; Therefore,

This is to give Notice,

That whosoever will pick them up will be rewarded for their trouble; but whosoever will conceal the above property, will be prosecuted according to Law.

Signed,

W. FINCH
Wm. JAMES
Wm. DAVIES
Thos. THOMAS

Cardigan, April 10th 1827.

I. THOMAS, PRINTER, CARDIGAN.

Despite the loss of life occasioned by the loss of the *Friendship* in 1827, her owners were keen to salvage what they could. (By permission of llyfrgell Genedlaethol Cymru/National Library of Wales)

Hebe

Date wrecked 6th September 1833
Type of vessel Yacht, 25 tons
Port of Registry Dublin
A pleasure yacht about 25 tons, called Hebe sailed from Milford Haven on Thursday belonging to a Mr Hargrave with his wife and five children (consisting of three fine young women, a son of about twelve or thirteen years of age and another daughter, younger) were on board and were seen that evening passing to the northwest by Jacks Sound by the Dove, revenue cutter. We are sorry to hear by a letter received yesterday by Mr Pritchard, of the Nelson Hotel, from a commercial gentleman (who with his wife were staying at the hotel when Mr Hargrave and his family were there) that they with the crew are all supposed to have been lost in the gale on Friday or Saturday for it is stated "a vessel was wrecked off the coast near Aberystwith and a lady washed on shore on Sunday about 9 miles to the westward [sic] of that place with her nightclothes and petticoat on, over which she had a gentlemans frock coat. Her linen was marked Elizabeth Ann Hargrave, she had on a pair of mens stockings marked John Hargrave, and a wedding ring on her finger. The body was deposited at Llanrhystud Church. A bed was also picked up 3 miles north of Aberystwyth marked J A Hargrave 1831, 16 Talbot Street (supposedly Dublin).
The Cambrian 6th September 1833

Lavinia

Date wrecked 5th September 1834
Built Aberdeen, 1817
Type of vessel Snow, 182 tons
Port of Registry Newcastle
Cardigan 09.09 " Lavinia of Newcastle leaving Aberaeron 5th inst struck outside the pier and sunk; her keel is gone and planks much chafed"
Despite this report that appeared in The Welshman and The Cambrian newspapers, *Lavinia* was eventually repaired, though according to her entry in Lloyds Register this was just one of a number of incidents in which *Lavinia* suffered serious damage.

Spread Eagle
Date wrecked 20 July 1835
Built Llanina 1814
Type of vessel Sloop, 30 tons
Port of Registry Aberystwyth
The closing entry in the shipping register for *Spread Eagle* reports her to have been lost at Craig-las, presumably delivering limestone or culm to the limekilns.

Star
Date wrecked 1st October 1836
Built Aberarth, 1807
Type of vessel Sloop, 32 tons
Port of Registry Aberystwyth
This vessel was lost with all hands on the night of 1st Oct 1836 between New Quay and Aberystwyth.

Lee
Date wrecked 3rd September 1840
Built Chester, 1825
Type of vessel Steamer, 188 tons.
Port of Registry Dublin
Aberystwyth Sept 7th – Picked up off the bar by the Pier boat, David Lewis, a raft containing one 17ft gang aboard, two 8 feet 6 inches board, supposed to be the top of a form, all painted green, having only a mark on the short form A, the form having been greatly repaired. Also on the same day several pieces of a wrecked vessel were picked up, supposed to belong to some Irish steamer. On Sunday last, a gentlemans hat was picked up on the beach and a ham as well as a quantity of candles. No information has yet reached us giving any authentic account of the supposed wreck though the following paragraph, which we copy from the "Shipping & Mercantile Gazette" of Monday doubtless refers to it... "The brig Echo, Evans from Newcastle, fell in with, on the 3rd instant at 6pm off Cardigan Bay the small steamer Lee from Cork for Liverpool, engines disabled, rudder head broken and the vessel leaky. The crew taken out and the steamer taken in tow by the Echo; about 9pm the hawser broke, and in consequence of the strong wind and heavy sea it was impossible to take one of the Echo's men out who was abandoned in the vessel." There is reason to believe that the mutilated remains recently picked up near Barmouth are those of this unfortunate man.
CDH 19th September 1840
The final resting place of the *Lee* will never be known but the balance of probability points to her having sunk somewhere along this stretch of coast. The story has a sequel in that the brig *Echo* was herself wrecked near Portaferry in December 1842.

Paquette de Bilbao
Date wrecked 14th January 1843
"Aberaeron Jan 14th Paquette de Bilbao from Liverpool for Cadiz was driven on shore this morning to the southwards of Aberystwyth, where she now lies high and dry, crew saved."
Nineteenth century regional newspaper accounts of shipwrecks were usually succinct and furnish

only the briefest details such as the above report from Liverpool Mercury, 20th January 1843. There were some newspapers that prided themselves on their coverage of maritime matters. The Carnarvon & Denbigh Herald, perhaps due to the many maritime connections within their circulation district, was one. From this source far more details of the wreck of the *Paquette de Bilbao* have been gleaned. The *Paquette de Bilbao*, Don Juan Antonio Gomez, master, was driven ashore near Llanon with loss of her rudder and mainmast cut away. She was a large vessel with a large number of hands on board. The noises made by the crew were heard at Morfa Mawr by Mr John Miller. He and his domestic servants, a great number of farmers and other inhabitants partially secured the vessel and valuable cargo (woollen cloths, hoop iron, steel etc) bound from Liverpool to Cadiz. The Spaniards were invited back to Morfa Mawr but thought they "were to be destroyed". The misunderstanding was sorted out by a young crewmember who spoke some English and they availed themselves of the hospitality offered.

Paquette de Bilbao was one of numerous ships lost around the coast of Britain at the time as a result of a hurricane, including two vessels making for Aberdyfi.

Perhaps because of the loss of the mainmast, none of the accounts state what type of vessel she was other than being a large Spanish vessel. The vessel was subsequently broken up.

Tamerlane

Date wrecked 23rd October 1846
Built St Martins, New Brunswick, 1824
Type of vessel Barque, 400 tons
Port of Registry Liverpool

At daybreak on the morning of the 23rd of October a barque was observed drifting some three and a half miles south of Aberystwyth. Immediately, the lifeboat was manned, horses put to the carriage and the lifeboat sent overland to render any assistance required. Before they could reach Morfa Bychan, the vessel drove up on the beach so high that the lifeboat was not required. The vessel proved to be *Tamerlane*, Captain Ackland from Liverpool to New Orleans. Her chain and anchor had parted hence the crew had been powerless to stop her drifting on shore with a south-westerly wind behind her.

Despite fears that she would become a total wreck, she was towed into Aberystwyth Harbour the next week and found to have little damage. An element of mystery clouds the proceedings at this point. Despite the relatively minor nature of the damage the owners were persuaded to sell the vessel along with her rigging and materials to local shipbuilder John Evans for a mere £200. After repairs and lengthening *Tamerlane* sailed from Aberystwyth for Quebec with 250 emigrants in May 1847. *Tamerlane* was named after a particularly bloodthirsty Central Asian Military leader of the middle ages.

Union Packet
Date wrecked 5th October 1852
Built Tenby, 1820
Type of vessel Smack, 29 tons
Port of Registry Milford Haven
With her sails in tatters and thus no means of steering the vessel it was evident to onlookers at Aberaeron that *Union Packet* was in deep trouble. She eventually came on shore, about a mile north of Aberaeron. Conditions were too rough to consider sending a boat out from Aberaeron harbour to save the crew. Instead, a boat was taken by horse and cart as close to the wreck as possible. From there four local sailors, at great risk to their own lives, ventured in a boat out to the wreck and the crew of *Union Packet* were safely landed but very much fatigued. Mr Cummins, landlord of the Feathers Hotel, had horses ready on the spot to convey the tired and bedraggled crew immediately to his hostelry where he treated them with the most remarkable hospitality. Initially the vessel was thought likely to become a total wreck. However as conditions ameliorated the *Union Packet* and her cargo of flagstones were saved.

Favourite
Date wrecked July 25th 1858
Built Wales, 1827
Type of vessel Smack, 33 tons
Port of Registry Cardigan
Aberaeron, July 25th. This morning at 2.30am the smack Favourite, Thomas, of Cardigan was stranded 200 yards west of this harbour and is likely to become a total wreck. Crew saved. She discharged limestones at Llangrannog yesterday and was bound for Milford; but last night it came to blow a gale from the westward, and she bore up for New Quay but could not fetch it. She anchored as near thereto as she could, and dragged both anchors, until she was nearly on shore: and the crew, four in number, slipped them in order to save their lives.
The Cambrian 30th July 1858

Despite the dire predictions as to the demise of *Favourite* she was eventually salvaged and shortly afterwards sold to Aberaeron owners. After repair she continued in the coasting trade under a new master.

Ardent
Date wrecked 8th December 1858
Official no. 12130
Built Newport, Pembs 1818
Type of vessel Brig, 138 tons
Port of Registry Aberystwyth
Reported to have struck a reef ten miles to the south of Aberystwyth and sunk without loss of life. *Ardent* probably struck the Cadwgan Reef just off of Llanon.

Frolic
Date wrecked 28th January 1867
Official no. 18570
Built St Dogmaels, 1857
Type of vessel Smack, 45 tons
Port of Registry Cardigan
Aberaeron, Jan 29th. The vessel

reported yesterday as being stranded was the Frolic, Thomas of and for Cardigan from Milford. She experienced during the passage thick and stormy weather, the vessel labouring heavily which caused her to leak and finding themselves to leeward and the vessel in a sinking state, they put up the signal of distress and ran for the beach. A boat, the property of John Miller esquire of Morfa Mawr, was launched and five seamen volunteered and pulled out through the heavy surf and rescued the crew, five in number and landed them safely on Morfa beach. The names of the volunteers are Thomas Price, David Owens, John Griffith, John Thomas and Evan Morris. The vessel is breaking up.
Shipping & Mercantile Gazette 30th January 1867
The register for *Frolic* confirms her demise, reading "Vessel totally lost at Llansantfffraed, Cardigan."

Little Liz

Date wrecked October 1870
Official no. 11439
Type of vessel Schooner, 75 tons
Built Plymouth, 1840
Port of Registry Fowey
During storm force winds blowing from the west north-west a vessel showing signs of distress was blown into Cardigan Bay. This came to the attention to Chief officer Berry of the New Quay coastguard who took no time in raising the life-boat crew. Once satisfied that the life-boat *Forester* was ready to attend the stricken vessel he arranged for the rocket apparatus (used for attaching a rope to distressed vessels) to be sent overland. However before either party could reach the vessel the crew could see disaster close at hand and took to the ships boat, landing safely at Aberaeron. Their vessel, *Little Liz*, followed them on to the beach at Aberaeron soon after where she was quickly wrecked. Under the command of Captain Hewitt *Little Liz* was bound from Glasgow to Bristol with a cargo of coal and pig iron. Fortunately for the crew of the local lifeboat a farmer loaned them three horses for their return to New Quay, saving them the row back.

Telegraph

Date wrecked 4th July 1875
Type of vessel Smack, 6 tons
Port of registry Aberystwyth
During the early part of the nineteenth century fatal accidents frequently befell fishing boats in Cardigan Bay. A melancholy incident involving the loss of two lives in 1875 must have seemed like a throwback to earlier times. Captain Richard Pugh of North Parade and Samuel Jones of Penmaesglas had set off from Aberystwyth harbour at 4am in the *Telegraph* to fish for mackerel. The weather was very rough and the boat encountered a stiff breeze. Whilst the men were adjusting the craft a sudden gust of wind carried away the foresail. This was seen by the crew of a fishing boat windward of the *Telegraph* at the time. Seeing her condition the vessel, under command

of Captain Phelp, immediately hastened to the assistance of the men. The crew of the fishing smack offered to take the *Telegraph* in tow to Aberystwyth. Pugh and Jones however refused any help and made for Llanrhystud into a strong south south-westerly wind. The crew of the fishing smack kept a lookout for the boat but eventually lost site of it. Concerned about *Telegraph* the smack returned to the spot where it was last seen but could find no trace of her. It is supposed that after Pugh and Jones lowered the foresail a second time the boat fell broadside to the wind, a squall came while she had no sail on and capsized her. The boat went down in ten fathoms of water. The yacht *Pearl* owned by Captains Richards and Morris was also cruising in the bay at the time but being a considerable distance leeward of *Telegraph* it could not approach the craft. At one time a rumour was briefly circulated in the town that the boat had arrived safely at New Quay together with the crew. Sadly this was not to be. Captain Pugh was a single man and his loss was deeply regretted by his numerous friends. Samuel Jones left a wife and five children to mourn his loss.

Briton
Date wrecked 1st Sept 1883
Official no. AB186
Type of vessel Fishing boat, 3 tons
Port of Registry Aberystwyth
Early on a Saturday morning Captain Thomas Thomas and a young neighbour David Jones, both of Victoria Street, Aberaeron, set off in *Briton* to go mackerel fishing along with two other boats, *Ella* and *Red Rover*. The wind at the time was blowing from the southwest. The other two boats came in during the course of the day but by 6pm the wind had veered to the south southeast and *Briton* could be seen some 3 miles offshore. About this time a squall descended and *Briton* was obscured from view. Never seen again, *Briton* was thought to have been sunk by the squall with the loss of two lives.

Martha Jane
Date wrecked 8th September 1903
*Official no.*44737
Built Aberaeron, 1862
Type of vessel Smack, 29 tons
Port of Registry Aberystwyth
The smack Martha Jane, owned and commanded by Captain Jenkin Jones of Aberarth was totally wrecked on Craig-las beach, just by Llanrhystud on Thursday night in last week. The cargo had duly been unloaded and the vessel sailed from the beach on Thursday but failed to reach Aberaeron harbour. She had under stress of weather to turn back to Craig-las beach. The wind veered to the north at about 9 pm on Thursday, just at full water bringing in heavy seas from the channel, which eventually frustrated the gallant attempts of the crew to save the vessel. Subsequently she was cut up into suitable lots and sold by auction. The timber was in excellent condition. She

was one of the vessels built beyond the limits of 25 years back at Aberaeron
Cambrian News 18th Sept 1903

Martha Jane on the beach at Llanrhystud shortly before her conversion into firewood.
(courtesy Amgueddfa Ceredigion)

Seven Brothers
Date wrecked 27th November 1909
Official no. 56213
Built Llansantffraed 1867
Type of vessel Schooner, 59 tons
Port of registry Beaumaris
With 84 tons of coal stowed in her hold *Seven Brothers* left Cardiff Docks on 17th November for Aberaeron. After sheltering in Milford Haven for nine days due to inclement weather *Seven Brothers* hove in site of her destination after making good use of a stiff breeze from the southwest. Taking advantage of the flood tide prevalent she ran for Aberaeron harbour under easy canvas. When approaching the harbour entrance the vessel was struck by a heavy sea on the starboard side, pushing her off course. She veered northwards and refused to answer to the helm and drove ashore. As the tide continued to come in the hull of the vessel was grinding and bumping against the boulders that comprised part of the sea defences. Waves broke constantly over the vessel. Relief came only as the tide receded. After enduring nearly two hours of this the crew set off emergency flares but as the tide ebbed they were able to climb down on to the sea defences without assistance. All the crew could do to try and save their vessel was to unload what they could of the cargo, estimated at 24 tons. The vessel was badly strained as a result of her stranding.
Seven Brothers was subsequently bought by Mr W J Phillips (to whom the cargo of coal was originally consigned) and cut up for firewood.

Seven Brothers getting well acquainted with the sea defences at Aberaeron, 1909.

M A Evans
Date wrecked 7th December 1904
Official no. AB22
Type of vessel Smack, 2 tons
Port of Registry Aberystwyth
Owned by local fisherman David Evans, *M A Evans* was wrecked on the beach at Llanon.

James
Date wrecked 5th November 1910
Official no. 29670
Built Cardigan, 1864
Type of vessel Schooner,25 tons
Port of registry Cardigan
Aberaeron – Stranded. The schooner James of Cardigan attempted to enter the harbour on Saturday night last between eight and nine o'clock but she was carried too far on the north side of the harbour before she was able to run her course properly. Consequently the vessel was run into the beach about 200 yards from the mouth of the harbour and there she lies. She had a load of coal for Captain Williams, Bridge End House. We are glad to state that the vessel is not much damaged. About twelve months ago another vessel was run ashore at the same point and was in consequence, obliged to be cut up for firewood.
Welsh Gazette 10th November 1910

James was more fortunate than her predecessor *Seven Brothers* and was successfully salvaged.

Guiding Star
Date wrecked 25th December 1926
Official no. 73582
Built Killinpike,1875
Type of vessel Schooner, 90 tons
Port of Registry Padstow
The site that befell a bleary eyed farm hand at Tregynan near Llanrhystud on Christmas morning 1926 told little of the drama that had unfolded further north in Cardigan Bay over the preceding days. His gaze fell on a schooner rigged vessel with sails set far out in Cardigan Bay and barely visible through the mist. He kept the vessel under observation for a time and noted it's erratic and lurching course but could detect no signs of life aboard. Eventually the vessel grounded on the rocks near Monk's Cave. The coastguards at New Quay were contacted and were on the scene in two hours. They were able to identify the vessel as the 96ton top rigged schooner *Guiding Star,* a Plymouth registered vessel built in 1875 and carrying a part cargo of basic slag. The bulwarks were badly damaged and the ships boat was missing. Hardly had observers noted any similarities to the *Marie Celeste* when news reached Aberystwyth of the safe arrival of the crew at Aberdaron. This had been achieved after a row of six hours in the ships boat. So exhausted were the crew that on landing they had fallen asleep either on the beach or in the boat.
Their troubles had started the preceding Wednesday when bound for

Par in Cornwall from Birkenhead. *Guiding Star* sprang a leak during the night necessitating Captain Bryant, his sons Cecil and Russell and crewman J Swanwick to man the pumps. Despite backbreaking hours of pumping their efforts were fruitless, had no impact and the vessel sank lower and lower in the water. With all now suffering from the intense cold and the decks awash Captain Bryant and his crew took to the ships boat. Owing to the misty conditions land was not visible but using their compass and knowing their position some fifteen miles from land they took to their oars. Villagers from Aberdaron roused the men the following morning and rendered them assistance. The following Monday Captain Bryant and his son Russell arrived in Aberystwyth to conclude formalities with the Receiver of Wrecks. Attempts had been made previously to salvage *Guiding Star* by pulling her off the rocks, most notably by T Hugh Jones of Aberystwyth. However the vessel was too well embedded and became a total wreck.

In early February an auction took place on South beach of chains, blocks, lamps, sails spars *et al* salvaged from the wreck before she finally broke up

"Messrs Rees & Evans have received instructions to sell by public auction on Thursday 10th Feb 1927 a quantity of salvaged goods from the wrecked schooner "Guiding Star" comprising chains, blocks, lamps, sails & spars etc. On view morning of sale at 2.30 pm prompt. Terms – Cash"
(*Cambrian News* 4th February 1927)

Graceful to the end *Guiding Star* sinks gradually below the waves near Monk's Cave, 1926.
(By permission of Llyfrgell Genedlaethol Cymru/National Library of Wales)

CHAPTER 4

Aberystwyth

The pattern of shipwrecks around Aberystwyth mirrors the growth and development of the harbour. As the nineteenth century progressed, the types of vessel visiting Aberystwyth changed and therefore so did the nature of those coming to grief. Much of the harbour trade in the early nineteenth century revolved around small sloops and smacks, used for herring fishing during the late summer and autumn, then for coastal trading the remainder of the year. Once the harbour had been improved during the late eighteen-thirties the number and size of vessels increased. Schooners, brigs and barques became a common sight anchored off Aberystwyth, waiting for the tide to bring sufficient water to cover the harbour bar and allow them passage into the harbour. This backdrop of steady development throughout the nineteenth and early twentieth centuries could not prevent the numerous tragedies that are a sad fact of life on the coast. These involved local fishing boats and more often than not took place at the harbour entrance, only a stone's throw from safety. Occasionally distressed vessels of greater size, and interest, would be blown over from the shipping lanes far out in St Georges Channel, grinding and juddering to a halt on the unwelcoming rocky coast. If the vessel could not be floated off anything salvaged would be sold off by public auction as soon as possible. Thus, as well as being an absorbing topic of conversation, the demise of a sailing vessel could also provide both a social event and rich pickings for anyone with an eye for a bargain (or, for that matter, anybody with light fingers if they could get to the wreck soon enough).

Once Aberystwyth became connected to other parts of the United Kingdom by rail the need for goods to be transported by sea diminished. The harbour saw less trade and the revenue from harbour dues declined. This in itself led to the destruction of *Fairy* in 1879. In addition, the Merchant Navy Act of 1870 saw the introduction of the Plimsoll Line, a simple device that prohibited overloading, and must have prevented countless shipwrecks, saving thousands of lives.

It was not unusual for pieces of wreckage to be washed up on the shores of Ceredigion and the Aberystwyth area was no exception. When the stern of a boat, marked *Charlotte* in yellow letters was washed up on the beach on January 25th 1840 much conjecture as to the demise of the vessel took place. In fact the wreck was not local at all. *Charlotte* had stranded on the 'Kentish Knock' and gone to pieces shortly afterwards, the crew escaping with their lives and little else. The wreckage had been washed from the English Channel, along the south coast of Britain and into Cardigan Bay in the space of three weeks. Part of a water cask bearing the inscription *Ocean Br...*, also boards, part of a bulwark and a ship's companion were washed up at Aberystwyth in early January 1843. The wreckage gave the appearance of having been in the water for quite a while. This vessel, perhaps *Ocean Bride* or *Ocean Breeze*, does not appear as a casualty in local shipping registers or in Lloyds Register of Shipping and remains something of a mystery. Flotsam again caused excitement on October 20th 1862 when a lifebuoy marked *Azores of Newport* was washed ashore opposite the Marine Terrace and caused a great deal of speculation. It had apparently been but a short time in the water as it appeared to be new and lately painted, also fragments of wreck had been cast ashore both to the north and south and it was feared that a vessel had been wrecked on the coast nearby. In fact, the wreckage had been in the water since the middle of September, when the 241-ton brig *Azores* foundered 25 miles to the north east of Cape Cornwall. *Azores* was built in Thomaston in Maine, USA, in 1847 but had been registered at Newport, Monmouthshire since 1859.

The twentieth century has seen only a handful of incidents, most involving fishing boats.

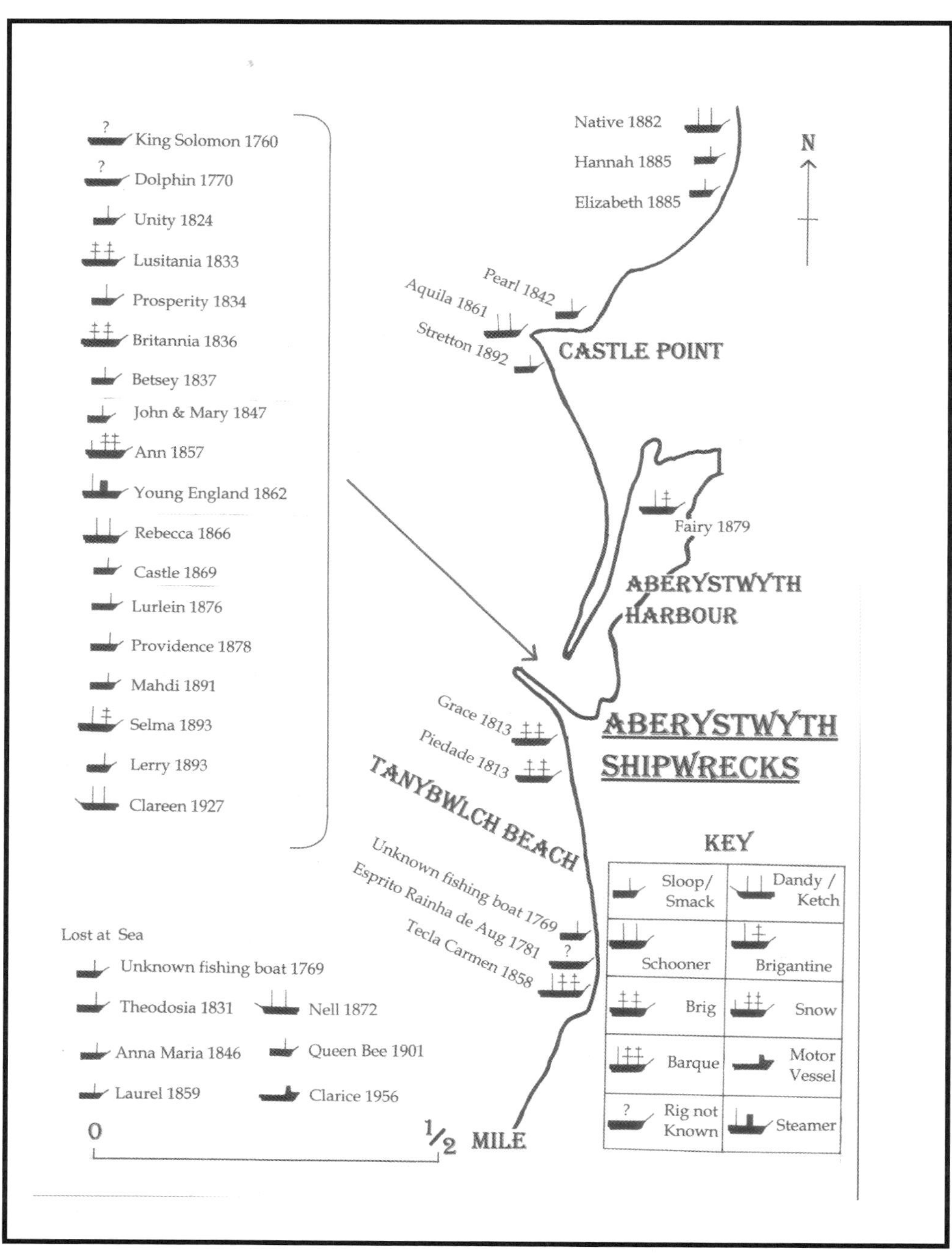
King Solomon 1760
Dolphin 1770
Unity 1824
Lusitania 1833
Prosperity 1834
Britannia 1836
Betsey 1837
John & Mary 1847
Ann 1857
Young England 1862
Rebecca 1866
Castle 1869
Lurlein 1876
Providence 1878
Mahdi 1891
Selma 1893
Lerry 1893
Clareen 1927
Native 1882
Hannah 1885
Elizabeth 1885
N
Pearl 1842
Aquila 1861
Stretton 1892
CASTLE POINT
Fairy 1879
ABERYSTWYTH HARBOUR
Grace 1813
Piedade 1813
ABERYSTWYTH SHIPWRECKS
TANYBWLCH BEACH
Unknown fishing boat 1769
Esprito Rainha de Aug 1781
Tecla Carmen 1858
KEY
Sloop/ Smack
Dandy / Ketch
Schooner
Brigantine
Brig
Snow
Barque
Motor Vessel
Rig not Known
Steamer
Lost at Sea
Unknown fishing boat 1769
Theodosia 1831
Nell 1872
Anna Maria 1846
Queen Bee 1901
Laurel 1859
Clarice 1956
0
1/2 MILE

An Aberystwyth victim of the *Royal Charter* Gale, 1859.

King Solomon

Date wrecked 1760?

During a meeting on 18th October 1760 of Aberystwyth Court Leet, (a forerunner of the Corporation of Aberystwyth) "The hull of the Dutch vessel *King Solomon* decreed to be a nuisance." This is thought to be a Dutch vessel that got into difficulties entering the harbour. At the time Dutch vessels were not infrequent visitors to Aberystwyth to collect cargoes of lead ore.

Dolphin

Date wrecked 18th Feb 1770

"The Dolphin, Turner, from Barcelona & c. for Chester was drove on shore in the late storm of the 18th inst near Aberystwith in Cardiganshire and immediately filled with water but most part of the cargo is got off and they are in hopes of saving the ship."

LL, Friday March 2nd 1770

Esprito Santa Rainha de Aug

Date wrecked May 1781

"master Fruz laden with Salt, Wine, and figs is on the shore at Aberystwith. The cargo will be saved."

LL, 15th May 1781

Unknown fishing boats

Date wrecked 3rd December 1789

Type of vessels fishing boats

Port of registry Aberystwyth

These two fishing boats were both caught out by the same storm. One overturned near Ffos-las to the south of Morfa Bychan. The second capsized near Aberystwyth. Altogether, twelve fishermen lost their lives.

Grace

Date wrecked 7th Sept 1813

Type of vessel Brig, 112 tons

Built 1793

Port of Registry Workington

On the morning of the 7th inst during a tremendous gale of wind two brigs were observed in great distress about two leagues from Aberystwith; soon afterwards one ran on shore near the bar of that port and proved to be the Grace, Fitzgerald from Liverpool to Waterford, with sundries – she fell on her beam end, went to pieces and her cargo is nearly all lost. The other went ashore and an hour after her companion: she was the Piety, Piers [Piedade, Perez] from the Brazils to Liverpool, with cotton; and her cargo was saved but much damaged. Both crews are safe.

Cambrian Sept 18th 1813

Piedade
Date wrecked 7th September 1813
Built Portugal
Type of vessel Brig

Piedade, Perez from Meranham for this port was driven on shore near Aberystwith 7th inst, cargo discharging and the Grace, Fitzgerald hence for Waterford was totally lost at the same time.
Liverpool Mercury September 17th 1813

The wreck of the *Piedade* on the same day as that of *Grace* is the most comprehensively documented account of a shipwreck on the Ceredigion coast during the early nineteenth century. This is due both to newspaper accounts and the arrival in Aberystwyth of William Daniell and Richard Ayton. William Daniell (1769-1837) was already a noted artist and was travelling around Great Britain with his companion Ayton. Their travels were to be published as "A Tour through Great Britain." Their journey around Britain was conducted sporadically over a period of years, the book being published in eight volumes between 1810 and 1825.

Of Aberystwyth he writes;

The hulk of the Piedade on shore at Tanybwlch. Alltwen can be seen in the distance.

"The entrance to the harbour is well sheltered but the entrance is exceedingly dangerous. This fact was brought to our conviction by the sight of a stranded vessel which had been wrecked in a gale that blew when we were in Tenby, and was lying on a bank of pebbles close to the harbour mouth, with one of her sides battered from stem to stern and with her masts, and sails, and rigging scattered in dismal ruin about her. She was a Portuguese ship from the Brazils, bound for Liverpool, and had been surprised by the gale, when she was so near to the land that no exertions could keep her off the shore. We understand that had the captain been acquainted with the nature of the harbour, she might, as there was at that time an unusual depth of water, possibly have been saved; but there is nothing that can indicate to a stranger its proper channel, which is so narrow, that in

bad weather it requires the utmost skill of the most experienced pilot to guide a vessel into it with safety. A small brig from Ireland was wrecked at the same time and nearly on the same spot; but she was so completely dashed to pieces that we saw few fragments of her remaining. The crews of both vessels were saved; but the cargoes of both were entirely lost.

The crew of the Portuguese ship were still at Aberystwith when we were there, and I was attracted by a little crowd to the door of a miserable kind of outhouse into which they were all crammed, to the number of eight or ten, and in a state of ineffable filth and wretchedness. There was a large fire on the ground the smoke from which diffused itself in a thick fog all over the place, and through this medium I could just distinguish a strange confusion of trunks and lumber from the wreck, and the men, some smoking, some sleeping, and some cooking with a host of monkeys screaming and chattering about them, and all jumbled together in a hole not more than twelve feet square. Their lodging here was probably in no degree worse than the forecastle of their vessels; but certainly common humanity required that the inhabitants of the town should have given people, and especially foreigners, who had just escaped from the horrors of shipwreck, a more hospitable reception".

Source: *'A Voyage Round Great Britain'* by Wm Daniell and Richard Ayton.

Unity

Date wrecked 26th Oct 1824
Type of vessel Smack
Port of registry Aberystwyth
Having been out overnight fishing for herring *Unity* was making her way back to Aberystwyth harbour in the early hours when she was overtaken by a violent storm. She was forced onto the bar at the harbour entrance and wrecked with the loss of seven lives. The inquests of the unfortunate fishermen are to be found in the Cardigan Gaol Files.

Theodosia

Date wrecked 8th Sept 1831
Built Bristol, 1820
Type of vessel Sloop, 11 tons
Port of registry Aberystwyth
Although built in Somerset, *Theodosia* was a sloop typical of those to be found around the west coast of Wales at this time, being carvel built with a running bowsprit, square stern, no galleries, no figure head, one deck and one mast. She was 27ft 10 ins long, 9ft 7 ins in breadth with a depth in her hold of 5 feet 1inch. Her crew would probably have consisted of the master, one crewman and a ships boy.

This vessel is recorded as being totally lost near Aberystwyth, her register not being saved.

Lusitania

Date wrecked 14th Sept 1833
Type of vessel Brig
The brig Lusitania from Quebec was on

shore at the entrance to Aberystwith on Saturday 14th inst. The cargo (timber) is expected to be saved.
The Cambrian 28th September 1833

Despite this report also appearing in Lloyds List it has not been possible to ascertain the subsequent fate of *Lusitania.*

Prosperity
Date wrecked 13th Dec 1834
Built Derwenlas, 1809
Type of vessel Sloop 70 tons
Carrying a cargo of Newport coal *Prosperity* approached Aberystwyth harbour in a stiff west south-westerly breeze accompanied by a ground swell. On approaching the harbour entrance she struck the bar and grounded. Although the vessel could not be saved most of the cargo was salvaged.

Britannia
Date wrecked March 1836
Type of vessel Brig
Port of Registry Swansea
The brig Britannia of Swansea, Gilbert, master is on shore behind the pier at Aberystwyth and is likely to become a total wreck - crew and materials saved.
The Cambrian, 12th March 1836

Betsey
Date wrecked 4th April 1837
Built New Quay, 1805
Type of vessel Sloop, 36 tons
Port of Registry Aberystwyth
Betsey had already had one lucky escape from destruction. During a storm ten years earlier her master drove her ashore on the sands at Borth to prevent her being wrecked on a less hospitable part of the coast. However her luck eventually ran out on Aberystwyth Harbour bar a decade later.

Pearl
Date wrecked Sept 1842
Type of vessel Smack
Port of registry Pwllheli
This vessel, commanded by Captain Parry, broke free from her moorings and was driven out to sea where she became a total wreck on Castle Rocks. To alleviate the loss suffered by Captain Parry, a subscription fund was set up in Aberystwyth, which was described by *The Welshman* newspaper as "going on favourably."

Anna Maria
Date wrecked Sept 1846
Built Tywyn, 1806
Type of vessel Sloop
Port of Registry Aberystwyth
Aberystwyth-Shipwreck. The sloop Anna Maria, Williams, from Neath, working up the Bay, on Thursday last, sprung a leak, and during the night went down about two miles south of this harbour. Crew saved.
CDH 26th September1846

John & Mary
Date wrecked 9th February 1847
Built Borth, 1842

Type of vessel Sloop, 44 tons
Port of registry Aberystwyth
Aberystwyth – Awful shipwreck and loss of lives. On Wednesday 9th inst about eleven in the forenoon, a vessel was seen approaching the harbour and when she neared it became visible that she was unmanageable. Hundreds of people gathered at the extremity of Rofawr, near to the entrance to the harbour. By this time the vessel had reached within ten yards of the beach and was knocked by the furious element on one side; the captain and crew took to the rigging where they remained for some time. The lifeboat was manned, but ere it could be of service, two of the men fell into the sea and were seen no more. The other two, a grown up person and a boy aged about sixteen stuck to the rigging, where they remained for a short time afterwards: still the unrelenting storm continued and they apparently had nothing before them but to share the fate of their comrades. One of them, the eldest managed to creep to the end of the mast and was laid hold by some of the persons on the beach and safely landed. The other poor lad cried aloud and stuck to the mast with all his might. By the time the lifeboat was placed between the wrecked vessel and the shore, and we must say no men acted more bravely. One of them, Richard Doughton, a young seaman not withstanding the violence of the storm succeeded in laying hold of the vessel and crept up her side and proceeded to the rigging to the almost exhausted lad took him in his own arm at risk to his own life, and with the help of other gallant tars landed him safely. Great credit is due to all the seamen. They did all in their power to save the whole of the crew, but we cannot close the painful narrative without mentioning the name of Jones, grandson of Lewis Morris Esq, late of Aberllolwyn. Mr Page the harbourmaster and Mr John Roberts, London House who exerted themselves in a praiseworthy manner. The vessel was found to be the John & Mary of Borth, laden with culm from Neath, Captain Evan Hughes, a young man of twenty-six years of age, who, as well as his mate perished in the storm. Their bodies have not yet been found. We shall present our readers with a more detailed account of the melancholy catastrophe in our next number.
Source: *CDH* 12th February 1848

John & Mary stuck on Aberystwyth harbour bar. The captain, seen suspended on a rope, is about to be suffocated by the cargo of culm cascading out of the hatches.
(courtesy Carmarthen Museum)

Ann
Date wrecked 3rd January 1857
Official no. 7692
Built Workington, 1810
Type of vessel Snow
Port of Registry Workington
Misjudging her approach to the harbour during a gale *Ann* became stranded at the harbour entrance. The gale increased in ferocity and at the height of the storm *Ann* went to pieces. A contemporary newspaper account mentions that most of her unspecified cargo was saved. *Ann* was quickly disposed of at auction four days later. An account book kept by farmer Evan Watkins of Moelcerni farm near Borth survives in the National Library of Wales. This notes that on Jan 7th he attended the sale of the wreck of the *Ann* of Workington in Aberystwyth. He purchased various lots including timber that cost £3 0 6d. His accounts included loaning a boy his own steed to send for a horse and cart from Moelcerni to take away his purchases. The boy earned sixpence for his efforts.

Tecla Carmen
Date wrecked 9th March 1858
Built Spain, 1857
Type of vessel Barque, 285 tons
The sight of a copper bottomed brightly painted new looking barque flying the Spanish flag firmly aground below the cliffs at Alltwen caused a sensation in the town of Aberystwyth on the morning of 9th March 1858. Rumour and counter-rumour flew around the town, further fuelled by the revelation that she was totally deserted, her charts, telescopes and even the crews personal effects were all in their appointed places. No attempt seemed to have been made to save anything and all three of her boats were still aboard the vessel. The fact that she was copper bottomed indicated that she was intended for sailing in tropical waters. Further examination revealed that her holds contained a small quantity of iron ore. Amongst the ships papers was a letter that shed some light on the vessel. The letter was addressed to Captain Aranna of the *Tecla Carmen* recently arrived at Falmouth. It was a reply sent in response to a telegram sent by the captain announcing his arrival at that port. It read "We have received a letter from our friends Draker, Rheimnant & Cohen, London by post, of which the following is a copy:- "We are obliged by your telegram advising arrival of the *Tecla Carmen* and we beg you to instruct the captain to proceed to Bristol, delivering his cargo at that port to Messrs Belve & Co." Customs invoices showed her to have sailed from Havana in Cuba with a cargo of sugar. After discharging her cargo at Bristol she loaded a quantity of iron ore to act as ballast on February 27th and sailed for Liverpool. Packages aboard the vessel suggested that she was to sail from Liverpool back to Havana.

Further examination of the vessel revealed damage on the port side commensurate with a collision. The full story was to emerge with the arrival of the 1133 ton American vessel *North American* (built Newcastle, Maine in 1831) at Liverpool carrying a cargo of cotton from Mobile. It seemed that the *North American* loomed suddenly out of the dark March night and bore down on the much smaller *Tecla Carmen* twenty miles or so from Bardsey Island. Crashing into her port side the vessels were locked together. The captain and crew of the *Tecla Carmen* believed her to be sinking and scrambled aboard the *North American* abandoning *Tecla Carmen* to her fate. Unfortunately no account of the discourse between the two captains remains though one suspects it to have been more than fiery.

On arrival at Aberystwyth to inspect the *Tecla Carmen* Captain Arannas announced dramatically that a quantity of gold and other valuable items were missing from the wreck. If the gold ever existed was it removed by an early bird local salvor? Or was it perhaps removed by one of the Spanish crew before the vessel was abandoned? Alternatively, did one of the crew of the *North American* purloin the gold on a speculative reconnoitre when the two vessels were locked together? Alas, it seems the riddle of the missing gold will always remain a mystery.

A court case reported in *The Carnarvon & Denbigh Herald* in May 1858 showed that gold was not the only precious metal to disappear from the wreck. Richard Doughton, a marine store dealer, was charged with having in his possession a quantity of copper which was allegedly stolen from the wreck of *Tecla Carmen*, now the property of W S Crealock Esq and George Green, who purchased the wreck at auction.

The copper seized was produced by a police officer and Mr Green produced a quantity of the same material belonging to the vessel to be compared with it. The similarity was stated as “very great”. Identification was also attempted by means of certain marks on a bolt found amongst the copper in dispute.

The three magistrates concluded that identification of the property was not so established as to warrant them to call upon Mr Doughton to reveal who had sold him the copper and the case was dismissed. Mr Green complained that several hundred weights of copper had been stolen from the wreck since it became his property but “...unfortunately the delinquents had hitherto eluded detection”. Before the sale of the wreck similar thefts were reported on a much more serious extent. It seems that the tradition of plundering shipwrecks on the coast of Ceredigion was not wholly consigned to the past.

The full details of the collision were laid before the Admiralty Court a few months later and reported in the national press.

Admiralty Court, July 12 (Before Dr Lushington and Trinity Masters)
The *North American* – Damage
This was a damage suited promoted by the owners of the late Spanish vessel Tecla Carmen against the American vessel North American in consequence of a collision which occurred between 10 and 11 on the night of the 8th of March last about 20 miles off Bardsey in the St Georges Channel. The Tecla Carmen, 285 tons, was bound at the time of the accident from Bristol for Liverpool, in ballast. Her case was that the night being clear and a strong gale blowing from the NNW she was standing westward with her yards braced sharp up close hauled on the starboard tack, making about four knots an hour, burning a bright light at her bowsprit and keeping a good lookout; that the North American was seen about a mile distant on the port tack, bearing from three to four points on the port bow; that an additional light was put over the Tecla Carmen's port quarter and that she was kept on her course until a collision became imminent; that the helm of the Tecla Carmen was then put hard a-port and she was luffed up into the wind in order to avoid it, but the starboard bow of the North American struck the Tecla Carmen on the port side abreast of her fore rigging. The two vessels remained in contact for some time, and the master and the crew of the Tecla Carmen got on board the North American. The Tecla Carmen has since been driven ashore at Aberystwyth having become a total wreck. The North American, 1333 tons was on her way with cotton from Mobile to Liverpool. It was alleged on her behalf that the weather on the night of the accident was dark and cloudy, the wind north-west-by-north and squally; that she was heading north-east-by-north, being close hauled to the wind on the port tack and proceeding at a rate of four knots an hour and burning a bright light at her bowsprit, and keeping a good lookout; that the Tecla Carmen was seen, without a light at the distance of about quarter of a mile, about two points on the starboard bow; that the helm was immediately ported and the spanker lowered; that the Tecla Carmen, instead of keeping on her course, which would have taken her clear and to windward, starboarded her helm and that she consequently bore down upon the North American, the bowsprit of the Tecla Carmen passing under the bowsprit of the North American and striking her port bow. The evidence of a number of witnesses, many of whom were examined viva voce when the case was last before the court, was adduced in support of the respective cases of the two vessels.
Dr Addams QC and Dr Twiss QC today addressed the court on behalf of the Tecla Carmen: and Dr Deans QC and Dr Spinks on behalf of the North American. The court deferred its judgement.
The Times, 13th July 1858.

In a subsequent hearing the *North American* was adjudged to have been at fault.

Laurel

Date wrecked 26th Oct 1859
Type of vessel Smack
Port of Registry Amlwch
A ships boat painted green, bearing the legend "John Price, Amlwch" was washed ashore at the southern end of Tanybwlch beach along with the inner end of a bowsprit belonging to a smack and another piece of wreckage eleven feet long. This was found to be from the *Laurel* which it seems met a similar fate to the *Twin Sister* (q.v) during the infamous '*Royal Charter* Gale.'. St Eleth Church, Amlwch, has a memorial stone to John Price, aged 20, and his brother Thomas, aged 15, who died aboard the *Laurel.*

Aquila

Date wrecked 19th February 1861
*Official no.*16428
Built Penybont nr Machynlleth, 1833
Type of vessel Schooner, 53 tons
Port of Registry Aberystwyth
Total wreck of the Aquila of Borth at Aberystwyth. *Our pleasant beach from one end of Marine Terrace to the other presented an anxious scene of no ordinary interest and excitement on the afternoon of Tuesday last when after bravely battling with wind and waves as well as she could through the night the schooner "Aquila" Captain Enoch James from Saundersfoot to Aberdovey, cargo small culm came ashore on the Wig where she became a total wreck for anything she will be any good for but old timber.*
It seems that she encountered the storm first about midday on Monday and weathered it out notably until 8 o'clock at night when just off St David's Head the vessel then running under double reef, away went her mainsail top sail and topgallant sail all torn to ribbons and there she was left with only her little fore and aft sails to settle it with wind and waves as she could. It blew a hurricane with torrents of rain all night but through it she drifted undaunted, though all about her looked very ugly and not a morsel of food had entered the lips of those on board for more than twenty and four hours: till about midday on Tuesday she hove in sight of this town evidently not a little anxious to reach it as soon as her crippled state would allow. For a while it was not certain if she would make it in or be pushed past Craiglais and go to pieces. Eight men "Hearts of Oak" rowed out to her assistance and one John Elias Evans jumped aboard and clung like a cat to her side. The crew of the Aquila were about to give up due to exhaustion. The other men were David Edwards, John Jenkins, James Ross, Thomas Ross, James Thomas, David Kinsey and George Hughes. The boat rescued the crew. There was one casualty as they reached land. David Edwards an old sailor broke his collarbone. Afterwards the men were taken to the Belle Vue and treated by Dr Jones with much care and

kindness. Aquila was insured but not for her full worth. The incident led to the call for a lifeboat in the town, shortly after which a meeting was convened. Following the incident a total of £23 7s0d was collected and distributed as follows.
To George Hughes for going out 30 shillings [£1.50p]
And use of his boat 30 shillings
To John Elias Evans for his brave and daring conduct 30 shillings
To David Edwards for going out in the boat and in consideration of his having been injured £4
To the other five men who went out in the boat 30shillings each
To Mrs Owen Rees for having at imminent peril to herself gone into the sea and saved the life of one of the men when the boat capsized 16shillings.
To Thomas Fox, Thomas James, John Drion, John Jones & John Edwards for going out in the second boat 16s each
AO 23rd February 1861

Young England
Date wrecked 30th Sept 1862
Official no. 28608
Built Wellington Quay, 1860
Type of vessel Steamer, 39 gross registered tonnage
Port of Registry Aberystwyth
Young England was in the service of the Cambrian Steam Packet Company who ran a fortnightly service between London and Liverpool calling at Aberystwyth, Aberaeron, New Quay, Aberdyfi, Tywyn and Barmouth. Barely a fortnight after being registered at Aberystwyth disaster struck. Whilst approaching Aberystwyth harbour during an autumn gale, the engine room flooded extinguishing the fire in her boiler. Without power *Young England* was at the mercy of the wind and tide and was driven onto the piles at the harbour entrance where she quickly met her demise. All three crew were saved.

Rebecca
Date of wreck 25th March 1866
Official no 5664
Built Weymouth, 1830
Type of vessel Schooner, 40 tons
Port of Registry Bridgwater
Wreck in the Bay*. On Sunday at about midday a vessel was seen in the offing with all her sails set. It was evident she refused to obey her helm for she drifted rapidly towards the rocks opposite the Castle Hotel* [today the Old College]**.** *To save her from immediate destruction her anchor was cast but could gain no hold and she continued to drag towards the breakers. A rowing boat with four men was put out to tow her in the direction of the harbour and for three hours succeeded in keeping her bow turned towards the sea. About three o'clock however as she approached the bar the heavy swells caught her and she was run ashore. The tide was running heavily at the time and an attempt was made to reach her by four men in a small boat from the harbour. This boat however was so frail and light that on approaching Rebecca it was all but capsized so that two of the men in the*

boat were thrown aboard the vessel and the remaining two having lost all the oars were left at the mercy of the boiling water. Fortunately the boat was washed in with the tide and ran up, half full with water high up on the beach where the two men in her were extricated from their dangerous situation. During this time the seas were breaking with terrible violence over the stranded vessel from which a buoy attached to a line was thrown into the water. The buoy failed to reach the shore and returned with the receding wave. It was evident that the situation of those on board was becoming desperate as they were seen to throw up their arms and intimate that the vessel was parting. Only the lifeboat could then have survived in the heavy sea running and the lifeboat was not there. At this juncture a young sailor named Watkin Lewis, regarded as the champion swimmer of Aberystwyth stripped off and dashed in among the breakers and under the anxious eyes of hundreds of spectators succeeded in reaching the buoy and bearing it back to the shore. A line of communication was thus established to Rebecca and a boat drawn with comparative ease to and from the vessel and those on board saved. No praise is too lavish to bestow upon the conduct of young Lewis, to whose intrepid bravery, under God, is perhaps attributed the saving of nine human lives.

The vessel was the Rebecca, captain Henry Francis. She was laden with guano and was bound from Bridgwater to Waterford. She left the former port on Wednesday the 21st but having lost her main boom and becoming waterlogged she became unmanageable and so drifted towards the coast, propelled by a wind from the west. She soon became a total wreck. All that remained of her was sold on Thursday evening by auctioneer Mr G T Smith.

A subscription was set afoot during the week by Mr Stanley J Balcombe, owner of the Queens Hotel, to present Watkin Lewis with a testimonial. The list was at once filled up. The presentation, a valuable watch accompanied by an address was organised for the following Saturday afternoon in front of the Queens Hotel.

AO 31st March 1866

The presentation was duly made and a watch inscribed "Presented to Watkin Lewis in recognition of his bravery in rescuing the crew of the *Rebecca* wrecked at Aberystwyth on Sunday the 25th March 1866."

Castle

Date wrecked 24th December 1868

*Official no.*15807

Built Aberystwyth, 1803

Type of vessel Smack, 70 tons

Port of Registry Aberystwyth

On Christmas Eve *the gale was blowing heavily from the NE when the old smack "Castle" (Capt George Lewis) 70 tons burden laden with limestone from Skerries near Dublin in unwisely endeavouring to make the Aberystwyth harbour during a late on tide between seven and eight o'clock struck upon the bar and drove to the north side of the*

pier. The heavy seas striking her every minute told the tale of the fate of the vessel as her timbers cracked and creaked beneath their merciless and multitudinous blows. The danger of the crew was at once patent and the secretary of the Lifeboat Institution ordered the boat to the rescue. The boat was immediately manned by 13 gallant volunteers and was launched with a considerable amount of difficulty, opposite Terrace Road. After being twice stranded by heavy seas striking her on her weather bows she was got afloat and then the conquering creature "walked the waters like a thing of life" and in an inconceivably brief space of time not withstanding the number of oars snapped by the wildness of the waves reached the distressed vessel and rescued the crew, three in number, whom she conveyed to the harbour, amidst the loud cheers of hundreds of spectators. But the work of the lifeboat and its crew was not yet over, for the Aberystwyth Shipping Society in which the smack was insured, engaged the lifeboat to carry six men to the stranded smack in order to secure her by lines to the shore. The lines were securely fastened as it was thought, but in taking the men off again one fell into the sea and was with difficulty rescued. In rescuing this man the boat was hurled broadside on the beach, and it took several hours to get her off. Meanwhile, one man had been left in the smack, and a perilous berth he had of it till the untiring and never too highly to be praised exertions of the crew succeeded in rescuing him at daybreak on Christmas day. The injury done to the lifeboat is we understand, not very material. Some of her timbers are however crushed, and part of her rowlock carried away. The "Castle" became a total wreck before noon Christmas day.
AO 2nd January 1869

Nell

Date wrecked 19th November 1872
Official no. 22747
Built New Quay, 1835
Type of vessel Dandy, 38 tons
Port of registry Aberystwyth
Foundering of a vessel – the dandy rigged smack Nell, 38 tons Mr William Evans, master, the property of Mrs Elizabeth Williams of Aberystwyth foundered on Tuesday night Nov 19th in five fathoms of water, a mile and a half west of Aberystwyth harbour. The vessel was manned by three hands including the master and had on board a cargo of sixty tons of lead ore, shipped at Aberystwyth by Mr William Morgan, mine agent, consigned for Bristol. From the masters statement it seems that the smack sailed from Aberystwyth on Tuesday morning Nov 19th, the tide being high, weather fine and a light breeze blowing from the South East. The vessel was then tight and in good condition. At two pm the same day she was three or four miles from Cardigan Island, the sea was very heavy and the wind from the south south-east blowing a gale. The vessel

appeared to labour very heavily and on sounding the pump it was found she was making water fast. All hands at once worked the pumps, but the water increased and the vessel was put before the wind for Aberystwyth harbour. Between five and six pm the pumps choked and the wind died away and at ten o'clock she gave a heavy lurch and immediately sank, the master and crew having hardly time to jump into the boat with only part of their clothes. They arrived safely in the harbour. The vessel was built at New Quay in 1835 and was worth £266 and the value of the cargo was between £800 and £900.
Cambrian News 22nd November1872

Crew agreements for *Nell* record the crew at the time to be Capt William Evans, 28, of Aberystwyth; Richard Roberts 21, of Aberystwyth, mate and William Williams 17 of Aberystwyth, boy. Captain Evans had no masters certificate. The last half yearly crew agreement drawn up for the vessel on July 6th 1872 records that since that date three mates and a ships boy had all left the vessel – perhaps an indication that she was not in a seaworthy state.
One question that begs to be answered is why did the master insist on trying to bring the vessel back to Aberystwyth instead of putting in at Aberaeron?

Lurlein
Date wrecked 1st August 1876
Type of vessel Fishing smack, 14 tons
Port of Registry Liverpool
Stranded and lost with death of it's master (J Rowlands) in wind conditions Force 6 on Aberystwyth harbour bar.

Providence
Date wrecked 7th Oct 1878
*Official no.*17214
Type of vessel Smack, 25 tons
Port of Registry Fleetwood
At 4.30pm on a Monday afternoon the fishing smack *Providence*, owned by Captain Humphrey Owens, New Street, Aberystwyth was attempting to get into the harbour over the bar when she was driven by the violence of the sea onto the trap. A huge wave broke over her and filled the hold with water. The owner and crew had to take their chances and jump for it. All reached shore safely. For a long time the boats' timbers withstood the onslaught of the waves but one by one gradually succumbed. The vessel had 20 baskets of fish (representing three days catch) aboard and was worth about £150. Like most fishing smacks, *Providence* was not insured. The reason cited for the wreck was the number of large stones across the bar.

Fairy
Date wrecked 26th July 1879
Official no. 52765
Built Littlehampton, 1864

Type of vessel Brigantine, 229 tons
Port of Registry Aberystwyth
Probably no account of a shipwreck could be less dramatic than that which befell the *Fairy*. A three-masted brigantine built by shipbuilder Henry Harvey, she was purchased by Trefechan businessman John Jones in 1878. Whilst moored in the harbour, presumably undergoing repairs following a voyage to Spain, she fell to the twin perils of an unseasonal storm and local government neglect. Since the arrival of the railway to Aberystwyth in the 1860's, harbour trade had decreased dramatically. A knock on effect of this was that the harbour dues, and thus the money available to maintain the harbour, decreased accordingly. Consequently, a summer storm that should have had little effect caused a major incident when one of the mooring rings to which *Fairy* was attached gave way. *Fairy* broke loose and was damaged to the extent that she became unseaworthy and beyond economic repair. Subsequent court action saw John Jones obtain damages of £1300 from the council. *Fairy* was broken up in 1882.

Sea Gull
Date wrecked 16th August 1879
Official no. AB123
Type of vessel Fishing boat, 3 tons
Port of Registry Aberystwyth
Used primarily for herring fishing, *Sea Gull* came to grief on the harbour bar without loss of life.

Fairy Queen
Date wrecked 23rd May 1882
Official no. AB152
Type of vessel Smack, 4 tons
Port of Registry Aberystwyth
Fairy Queen, owned by John Edwards of 25 Pier Street, was wrecked on Aberystwyth's Castle Rocks.

Native
Date wrecked 24th November 1882
Official no. 47070
Built Aberystwyth, 1864
Type of vessel Schooner, 85 tons
Port of Registry Aberystwyth
A lively scene was witnessed in the bay of this town Wednesday afternoon. At midday a telegram was received from Aberaeron that a schooner labouring heavily was making for Aberystwyth and advising a lookout. Consequently Capt Tom Williams, coxswain, having seen that the lifeboat was ready for immediate service in case of need proceeded to the harbour to await events and here a large number of persons, chiefly sailors soon assembled. During this time the schooner was seen making towards the port under one yard and a jib, a stiff breeze blowing accompanied by a heavy sea and frequent showers. At about half past three the vessel, which was understood to be the Native of this port, with coal, came close to the harbour but the tide being not sufficiently high Captain John Thomas, harbour master had not put up the ball and flag and therefore the schooner hoisted an additional sail and tacked

out to sea again. It soon became evident to the spectators that the sails were damaged and that the vessel was not under complete control, for she seemed to steer around against the wind in order to get into the open sea. Meanwhile she was getting unpleasantly close to the Castle Rocks and it being decided by those watching at the harbour mouth that she would not return, a general run was made towards the Castle and Marine Terrace to render assistance if necessary. By this time the foremost of those had reached the Promenade Pier the Native was quietly sailing round like an ordinary pleasure boat and grounded. After some slight difficulty a rope was thrown from the ship and the anchor brought ashore. During the night a quantity of coal was discharged. She is still lying on the beach and only slightly damaged but a heavy sea is running *AO* 25th November 1882.

Native was indeed salvaged, the cost of repairs amounting to £200. Barely had these costs been recouped when *Native* was lost in January 1886 at Ardglass, Northern Ireland.

Providence
Date wrecked 25th Sept 1885
Official no. AB198
Type of vessel Smack
Port of registry Aberystwyth
Wreck of a fishing boat *– on Saturday morning the fishing boat Providence belonging to Mr Alfred Worthington junior struck on the stones near the harbour mouth and foundered. There was a fresh in the river and a heavy sea and the occupants of the boat, Mr Worthington and his son and John Hughes of Portland Lane with difficulty saved their lives. A large number of oil paintings are on view in Mr David Lewis's shop in Little Darkgate Street. The paintings are by Mr Worthington and are to be drawn for on the fine art principle, and proceeds being devoted to the repair of the damage done to the boat and nets. Some of the paintings are of real merit.*
CN 25th September 1885

According to the same source a fortnight later the money raised was sufficient to pay for the damage. The painting on the cover of this book is also by Alfred Worthington.

Hannah
Date wrecked 30th Sept 1885
Official no. AB223
Type of vessel Smack, 3 tons
Port of Registry Aberystwyth
Elizabeth
Date wrecked 30th Sept 1885
Type of vessel Smack
Port of Registry Aberystwyth
Destruction of fishing boats. *Tuesday evening at 8.40 pm a number of boats went out to fish for herring. However a storm blew up and most made it back to the harbour at daybreak. One had to run with the wind and beach at Clarach. Three boats were forced to anchor in the lee of the chain pier hoping the gale would*

abate. These were Elizabeth (Evan Jones), Hannah (William Edwards) and Harriet (John Cole). In the afternoon in obeyance to signals from the shore John Cole hoisted his anchor and ran his boat, which was smaller than the other two, ashore. She was then safely hauled up the beach. At 8 p.m. Hannah was swamped. Elizabeth rode the storm well but at 3a.m. on Thursday morning she too foundered. In a few hours the boats were beached but Hannah was cut in two and Elizabeth had gone to pieces. The nets were also greatly damaged. Sympathy is extended to their owners as this is the start of the fishing season.
CN 02/10/1885

Mahdi
Date wrecked 24th September 1891
Official no. AB5
Type of vessel Smack, 5 tons
Port of Registry Aberystwyth
Boat accident. *On Thursday morning of last week the Maddie (sic) mackerel and herring boat owned by Mr Edward Edwards and manned by him and Mr Morgan Hopton got into the trap at the harbour and was dashed to pieces. When the boat was coming into the harbour there was not only a flood in the river and a strong south-westerly wind but the Doctor Livingston was coming out of the harbour. The Maddie [sic] could not clear and a large wave carried her on to the piles where she went into the trap and was knocked to pieces. The boat was worth about £25. Subscriptions were solicited on Friday and Saturday and about £15 was obtained.*
CN 02/10/1891

Stretton
Date wrecked 27th October 1892
Official no. AB34
Built 1876
Type of vessel Dandy, 7 tons
Port of registry Aberystwyth
Stretton was wrecked on Castle rocks by a storm that also blew another vessel ashore on the main beach as well as damaging others.

Selma
Date wrecked 27th Sept 1893
Built Abo (Finland), 1866
Type of vessel Brigantine, 205 tons
Port of Registry Kalmar, Sweden
205-ton Swedish Brigantine wrecked at the harbour entrance. The paucity of details regarding the demise of *Selma* suggests that rather than being involved in any dramatic incident she misjudged her entry into Aberystwyth harbour suffering a great deal of damage. The wreck was disposed of shortly afterwards at auction.

Lerry
Date wrecked 18th December 1893
Official no. 56420
Built Ynyslas, 1871
Type of vessel Smack, 33 tons
Port of registry Aberystwyth
Monday 18th December 1893 dawned grey with a stiff gale blowing from the south-west and attendant rough seas. In the small hours the Aberystwyth &

Aberdovey Steam Packet Company's steamer *Countess of Lisburne* had entered the harbour safely bringing with it a variety of packets and consignments for the tradesmen of Aberystwyth. Captain Thomas the harbourmaster came to chat to the crew and make a note of the dues owed. Farther out he could see a one masted vessel, a smack, waiting for sufficient water and hopefully a lull in the blustery weather to enter the harbour. This was the 33 ton smack *Lerry* carrying a cargo of coal for Captain Doughton, retired sea captain turned coal merchant. *Lerry* was an Aberystwyth registered vessel built at Ynyslas in 1871 and owned by master David Davies of High Street. Also aboard was his son Edward and crewman John Henry Thomas, also of Aberystwyth. Having some concerns about the conditions Captain Thomas consulted with others of experience as to whether conditions were suitable for the smack to effect a safe entry. Shortly after one o'clock Captain Thomas raised the signal flag to let *Lerry* know there was sufficient water to enter the harbour. At first the prevailing south-westerly served to render the flag invisible from the *Lerry*. The flag was then taken from its pole and waved manually. Captain Davies set his gaff topsail and single reef mainsail and ran for the harbour. In the harbour entrance the hobble boat waited. Entry to Aberystwyth harbour requires a prompt turn through ninety degrees. This is no problem for a vessel with even an auxiliary engine but presents a potential hazard to any sailing vessel entering the harbour. Hence the need to attach a rope to the bow of a sailing vessel such as the *Lerry* in order to winch her round. *Lerry* negotiated the harbour bar safely but whilst in the following breakers the wind dropped suddenly leaving the vessel unmanageable. With the hobble boat unable to venture into the rough seas *Lerry* was now at the mercy of immense breakers, slowly but surely inching her on to the trap between the groynes on Rofawr. Breakers now smashed into the stricken vessel, rolling her about with immense force placing the crew in danger of their lives. It was now apparent to all those watching that carrying a heavy cargo as she was and with the constant battering of the waves it was only a matter of time before she broke up. John Henry Thomas had by now climbed to the top of the mainsail and was ready to take his chances by dropping down onto the beach. The crowd waiting on shore persuaded him otherwise. Two lifebelts had now been thrown to the exhausted but courageous crew aboard the *Lerry*. With one end of the rope being held by crew on the *Lerry* and the other by rescuers on land each crew member plunged into the surf and was dragged to safety.

By Tuesday morning the vessel was dismasted and breaking up fast. A brief respite at low tide allowed the unloading of six tons of coal. However the following tide pitched the vessel over exposing her deck to the sea. The remaining cargo was rapidly washed out and the vessel became a total wreck. *Lerry* was insured with the Cambrian Mutual Marine Insurance Society.

Queen Bee

Date wrecked 7th August 1901
Official no. AB231
Type of vessel Smack, 3 tons
Built 1895
Port of registry Aberystwyth
What had started off as a pleasant days sailing turned into tragedy as *Queen Bee* headed back for Aberystwyth. Whilst manoeuvring the boat in the direction of the harbour a wave swamped the stern of the boat and it quickly sank. Other boats nearby came to the rescue but were too late to save five of the party.

Jubilee Queen

Date wrecked 15th June 1912
Official no. AB19
Type of vessel Smack, 9 tons
Port of Registry Aberystwyth
Having been busily engaged in mackerel fishing off Aberaeron, the fishing boat *Jubilee Queen* came to the main beach at Aberystwyth to discharge her catch. Shortly after she was driven ashore and broke up. Her remains were briefly removed to the promenade where she swiftly became an object of curiosity to the thousands of visitors in Aberystwyth at the time. Her owner was William Williams of 6 Spring Gardens, Trefechan.

Jubilee Queen proves an unexpected attraction on the beach at Aberystwyth, 1912.

Clareen

Date wrecked March1927
Official no. 86521
Type of vessel Ketch
Built Plymouth 1884
Port of Registry Waterford
Boulders washed down the two rivers that merge at the entrance to the harbour have frequently caused problems for shipping at Aberystwyth. As *Clareen* approached Aberystwyth she hit one of these and was thrown off course. This in turn caused her to collide with the stone pier at the south side of the harbour. Either the boulder or the collision with the stone jetty had holed *Clareen* below the waterline. It was soon evident that she was taking in water. She was eventually moored against the quay where her cargo of sodden coal was unloaded. *Clareen* spent her last months as an unofficial playground for local children whilst her owners considered their options. They elected not to repair her and *Clareen* was broken up on the Trefechan side of the harbour.

Clarice

Date wrecked 29th July 1956
Official no. 87453
Type of vessel Motor vessel, 10 grt
Built Appledore, 1948
Port of Registry Cardigan

Abandoned as a total loss off Aberystwyth. A sudden north-westerly gale sprang up on the morning of 29th July 1956. A number of fishing boats were caught out but managed to battle their way into the harbour. Less fortunate was the *Clarice*. Jack Phillips, the skipper, chose to try and ride out the storm. As the weather deteriorated, *Clarice* started to take in water. The Aberystwyth lifeboat under coxswain Baden Davies first circled *Clarice* and then came alongside to take off the two crew. *Clarice* was left anchored with anchors and chain. Later she broke her moorings, capsized and was eventually dashed to pieces on the rocks between the castle and the pier.

CHAPTER 5

Clarach to Ynyslas and Patches

The stretch of coastline that stretches from north of Aberystwyth to the Dyfi estuary is one of contrast. The first six miles are a rocky and inhospitable coastline from which shipping is best served by keeping away. On this stretch there are two possible landing sites. The first of these is the sandy beach at Clarach, at one time used to load sloops with lead ore. Further back in time Clarach was the landing place used by the Vikings when they pillaged the area during the tenth century. Suprisingly, no accounts of shipwrecks at Clarach have come to light. However, occasional pieces of wreckage announcing disaster elsewhere have sometimes washed up. One such example was the stern of the *Adelia* which caught fire off Tuskar Rock near Rosslare in 1848. A short distance further on is the small isolated sandy beach at Wallog. Here occasional cargoes of limestone were unloaded and burned in the limestone kiln that dominates the beach. The most notable feature of Wallog is neither the sandy beach nor the limekiln but the ribbon of glacial moraine that stretches out into Cardigan Bay. A relic of the ice age, Sarn Cynfelyn carries on underwater for nearly seven nautical miles, terminating in an area of shallow water known as Patches. Its older, historic, name is Caer Wyddno. Sarn Cynfelyn has not claimed as many casualties as it's northern neighbour Sarn

Padrig but, nevertheless, it is a considerable hazard to shipping. If it were not for the benign nature of the seafloor, Patches would have seen far more casualties. One of the high- profile near misses on Patches was the Liverpool – Aberystwyth steamer *Plynlimon.* This vessel ran a regular service carrying both cargo and passengers. On 14th December 1858, whilst in the vicinity of Patches, she struck bottom causing an extensive leak in the hull. The vessel proceeded a short distance but the water soon rose sufficiently to extinguish the fire in her boiler. She was then forced to anchor, and the nervous passengers were rowed ashore by the crew. *Plynlimon* was then towed into the harbour to discharge her cargo and survey the damage. The following year the Liverpool registered *Queen* was seen grounded on Patches, disabled with both foretopmast and mizzenmast gone. She was also subsequently towed off.

Patches may also be the resting place of the *Pomona* of Dartmouth. The bodies of four of her crew, along with the ships boat, were found washed ashore at Wallog in April 1812. It is thought that the vessel hit one of the sandbanks in Cardigan Bay and the crew took to the ship's boat but were swamped as they tried to land. As there were no survivors from the wreck it is equally plausible that *Pomona* was a victim of Sarn Padrig.

Once the cliff line finishes at Upper Borth, the coastline takes on a different aspect. Three miles of golden sand extend up to Ynyslas at the mouth of the Dyfi estuary. There have been relatively few wrecks in this area despite its proximity to the busy port of Aberdyfi. The sandy beach was much kinder to distressed vessels, a fact sometimes acted on by vessels in peril. It was not unusual for vessels caught out in ferocious seas to head for Ynyslas and run their vessels aground in the soft sand. Examples include the brig *Renown* in November 1816 and the sloop *Betsey* in March 1827. During the *Royal Charter* gale in 1859, two vessels ran ashore at Borth in order to save themselves. There is a degree of irony that a beach offering relative safety for distressed vessels should be embroiled in one of the cruellest legends surrounding shipwreck in Ceredigion. The story came to light during an encounter between two fishermen at Aberystwyth harbour entrance in 1913. Narrowly avoiding collision as a Borth boat was leaving the harbour and a local boat about to enter it the Aberystwyth skipper railed at the other causing visible offence by use of the word 'Portuguese'. The witness to this event was no less than the Celtic scholar J Glyn Davies. Intrigued by the altercation, he sought out the Aberystwyth skipper. His curiosity was rewarded by the account given. This related to a shipwrecked Portuguese sailor who had the misfortune to be washed ashore at Borth. Not unduly concerned about the man's welfare the locals eyed up his leather boots and attempted to remove them. The boots, having swollen and so being difficult to remove, caused the locals to resort to hacking the poor man's legs off in their eagerness to acquire some new footwear. As he lay dying on the beach, the sailor is said to have cursed the inhabitants of Borth until the ninth generation. It is fortunate for us that Borth's inhabitants were sufficiently fluent in Portuguese to understand the poor mans last words.

The Dyfi estuary as a whole has seen numerous casualties, probably enough to merit a book on their own account. Only those on the Cardiganshire side of the estuary are detailed here. The *Moringen*, wrecked in 1897 provides the only, albeit occasionally, visible remains of a wreck known above the waves on the coast of Ceredigion. Under certain conditions stumps of her timbers can be seen protruding from the sand on the south side of the Dyfi estuary.

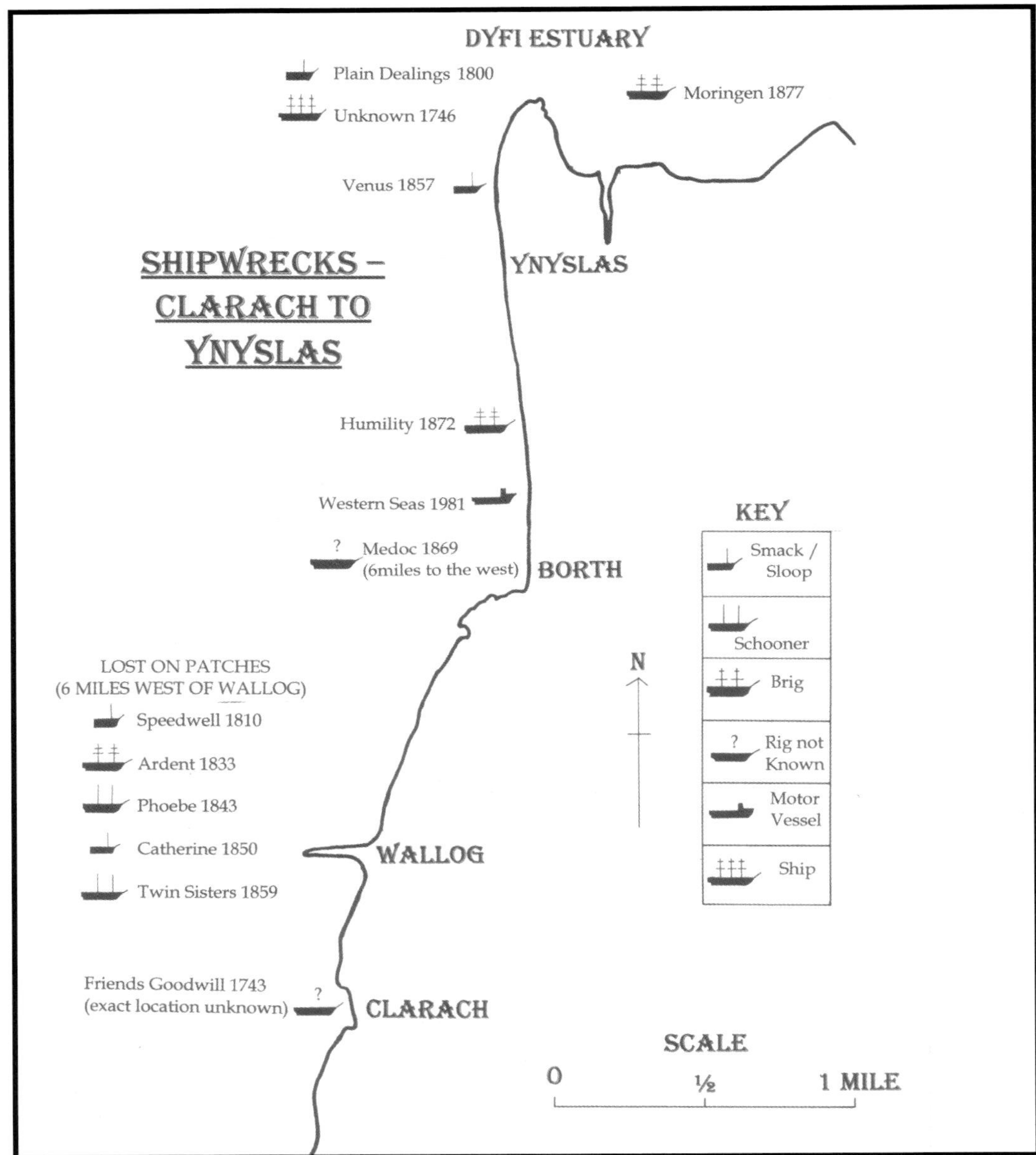

Friends Goodwill

Date wrecked October 1743

This vessel came to grief somewhere between Aberystwyth and Aberdyfi. Amongst the Nanteos estate papers is an account of the payments due to all those who assisted Captain Doulman to salvage the vessel and it's unspecified cargo. The total payments came to over £159 and included well over a hundred persons. Whether the wreck had been left to the mercy of the local looters or saved by going through official channels probably didn't make much difference once the final accounting had been finished.

Unknown Spanish vessel

Date wrecked 22nd November 1746

Type of vessel Ship

Dr David Jenkins served as Librarian at the National Library of Wales for ten years. During his childhood in Penrhyncoch he frequently heard a tale of how once the cellars and larders of nearby Plas Gogerddan were replenished when a Spanish vessel became a total loss at Borth. Many members of the crew, having managed to gain the shore, were so scared of the tempestuous sea that they settled in the surrounding districts where they found ready work in the local lead mines. This episode was generally quoted to explain the marked Spanish traits of a few local families.

It was therefore of particular interest to Dr Jenkins that when the Gogerddan estate papers were acquired by the National Library of Wales they were found to contain a small bundle of depositions by a few witnesses relating to the stranding of a Portuguese ship at Borth on "ye 22 day of nobr 1746 " and the resulting claims for salvaged goods. The evidence, sworn before Thomas Johnes of Hafod on 16 November 1749 states that David James, David Lewis, and Edward Williams, all of Borth helped to secure "severall puncheon of oyle, Lemons, Oranges, Chest Pomgranets, Ropes, corkwood and one saile... stranded on ye shore within the lordship of John Pugh Pryce " [of Gogerddan] and that these were later carried to Gogerddan. The witnesses asserted that they had delivered " ye goods for use of ye Lord [of the manor] John Pugh Pryce Esqr., to Mr David Morgan Deputy Agent [of the Gogerddan estate] who upon salvage received about ten pounds and Mr Richard Hughes five guineas. Neither of them took any trouble in secureing ye same from ye surface of ye Sea but took them to Gogerddan after they had been secured by Edward Williams and his assistants." A further note states that some of the shipwrecked sailors sought work in the local lead mines, which they procured.

The Gogerddan collection also contains a letter detailing activities on the Merionethshire side of the Dyfi. This refers to a large vessel in great distress entering the Dyfi estuary with only its mizzenmast standing. The inhabitants of Aberdyfi attempted to reach the vessel but due to the conditions could not reach them. The inhabitants of Aberdyfi could clearly see vast quantities of cargo coming on shore on the Cardiganshire side of the estuary and being freely removed by the local inhabitants in the presence of the Customs Officers. It seems likely that much of this booty was being taken to Gogerddan. The inhabitants of Aberdyfi sought to follow their example and salvaged three puncheons of oil, one cask of wine, some cork wood, some lumber goods with some boxes of lemons and oranges. These were taken to a warehouse owned by John Angell. The Merioneth Customs Officers then forced their way into the warehouse to seize the salvaged goods. This seeming to be in contrast to the actions of the Cardiganshire Customs Officers incensed the inhabitants of Aberdyfi. Their letter goes on to mention another wreck at Llanon where it seems Cardiganshire Customs Officers turned a blind eye and allowed goods to be carried away unmolested. However the inhabitants of Aberdyfi had it seems been forced to help Customs Officers on other occasions but received no reward for their efforts, adding to their sense of injustice.

Plain Dealings

Date wrecked 5th April 1800
Built Barmouth, 1790
Type of vessel Sloop, 39 tons
Port of Registry Barmouth
Although reported only as having been stranded near the mouth of the Dovey, the death by drowning of three of the crew suggests that the incident was of a more serious nature. The inquests of John Edward, Hugh Richard Hugh and Morris Williams were held in a public house at Tre'rddol.

Speedwell

Date wrecked April 1810
Type of vessel Sloop
Port of Registry Aberystwyth
Speedwell, (Charles Jones, master) was returning to Aberystwyth from Newry with a cargo of limestone. As well as the limestone, Speedwell had on board the crew of another Aberystwyth sloop the *Invincible*. During a gale on the 25th March, *Invincible* had failed to live up to her name and was wrecked on Bray Beach near Dublin. The remains of *Invincible* had been sold for £20. This money was now in the care of the returning crew. When near Patches *Speedwell* sprang a leak and rapidly filled with water. The two crews were able to launch the ship's boat and scramble in with seconds to spare before the sloop disappeared under the waves. There was no time to collect their spare clothes and personal belongings and these, along with the £20, went to the bottom of Cardigan Bay. Their plight was spotted by another sloop, *Sincerity*, who saw *Speedwell* go down and landed both crews safely back in Aberystwyth.

Ardent

Date wrecked 29th Feb 1833
Built Aberystwyth, 1816
Type of vessel Brig, 106 tons
Port of Registry Aberystwyth

Being a native of Aberystwyth, it was to be expected that Captain Evan Jones, master of *Ardent*, would have been familiar with the hazards of Cardigan Bay and acted accordingly. However, whilst sailing from Cardiff to Liverpool with a cargo of iron bars *Ardent* struck on Patches during a strong north north-westerly gale. The stern of the vessel was soon knocked in and *Ardent* wrecked. Fishermen were able to retrieve these iron bars from Patches for years after and sell them as scrap. Later Captain Jones opened a wine and spirit business in Aberystwyth at the corner of North Parade and Terrace Road, a site now occupied by Barclays Bank.

Phoebe

Date wrecked 14th October 1843
Built Newport, Pembs, 1839
Type of vessel Schooner, 123 tons
Port of Registry Cardigan

When the smack *Union*, of Aberaeron, arrived safely in the recently improved harbour at Aberystwyth, the captain and crew gave information that an apparently new vessel, a two-masted schooner had gone down near the Patches in their sight. The news spread rapidly through the town and mariners, visitors and townspeople headed to the Castle grounds with telescopes for the purposes of establishing if any of the crew were in the rigging, which was visible, and ascertained this to be the case. John Griffiths, a boatman, and four other young men took their boat about 11o'clock at night to the vessel. All perished. John Griffiths' body washed ashore at Borth along with his boat. The others were John Fisher, William Monks, John Morgan and Edward Watkins. A ship's boat, nearly new came ashore at Borth on Sunday belonging to *Phoebe* of Newport, registered at Cardigan. Masts and further wreckage came ashore at Aberdyfi. The weather in the days preceding the wreck had been very stormy, the Friday described as being a perfect hurricane complete with thunder and lightning. Following this tragedy a fund was set up to establish a lifeboat for the town. The sum of £96 was raised and with this money a six-oared boat for use in emergencies was provided for the harbourmaster.

Catherine

Date wrecked 4th February 1850
Built Llanelltyd, 1810
Type of vessel Smack
Port of Registry Porthmadog

The smack *Catherine*, David Evans master, was carrying an unspecified cargo from Newport, Monmouthshire, to Mochras. She left Milford Haven on 4th February in the company of other vessels bound for north Wales ports. She lost contact with these other vessels when abreast of Fishguard. All the other vessels were subsequently accounted for. It is supposed she hove to as the gale then blowing increased in intensity to a hurricane. Her eventual fate is open to conjecture, but it is thought she was blown on to Patches and there wrecked. The melancholy find of two Welsh bibles (one of which belonged to the captain) and a Welsh hymn book (belonging to the mate) on a nearby beach further strengthened this theory. Both Captain and Mate were married men. In Porthmadog a subscription fund was set up for the families of the two men.

Venus

Date wrecked 8th June 1857
Official no. 9834
Built Aberystwyth, 1805
Type of vessel Sloop, 41 tons
Port of Registry Aberystwyth

Following the loss of any vessel the crew were required to make depositions to the local Receiver of Wreck. Many of these from the late nineteenth and early twentieth centuries are to be found in the National Archives in Kew. Those for earlier dates are, however, quite rare. One that has survived is that of the *Venus* and is quoted here.

"22 June 1857. I, the above named Thomas Davies master & part owner of the above named vessel do hereby declare that on the 6th inst. From Carnarvon to Aberdovey with Limestones and that on the 8th about 5am blowing a strong gale from the Westward the peak tie chain parted whereby the vessel became unmanageable; there being only one hours flood at the time it was not safe to attempt Aberdovey Bar, being on a lee shore, and with a view of saving our lives and the vessel, I had no alternative but to run for the nearest beach which was effected about a mile to the south of Aberdovey Bar, seeing the vessel breaking up fast, I took to the sea, leaving the remaining three on board who all perished as the vessel soon went to pieces, after great exertion I landed in a very exhausted state."

Twin Sister

Official no. 20483
Date wrecked 26th Oct 1859
Built Wexford, 1857
Type of vessel Schooner, 91 tons
Port of Registry Lancaster

Presumed lost off Aberystwyth during the "*Royal Charter* Gale." One of her boats, marked *Twin Sister of Barrow, Wm. Porter,* master was picked up on the coast seven miles to the south of Aberystwyth. Carrying a cargo of coal from Newport to Liverpool she was last seen off Bardsey Island on the night of the storm. How the vessel and her crew met their fate will only ever be open to conjecture but with north-westerly hurricane force winds behind her it is possible that she was forced onto Patches and there broke up.

Medoc

Date wrecked 19th November 1869
Type of vessel 604 tons
Port of registry Bordeaux

St Patricks Causeway (west of Barmouth) has claimed many casualties over the years. When a vessel was seen to be in trouble on the causeway, the local lifeboat *Ellen* was rapidly launched into a fresh north-westerly wind. On her way to the stricken vessel she encountered the crew of seventeen men who had abandoned the vessel, taken to the two ships boats and were now heading for land. Fortunately, the lifeboat intercepted the two boats prior to reaching the approaches to the broken water before the bar at the mouth of the Mawddach Estuary. Taking some of the sailors from the overcrowded boats *Ellen* was able to assist the remaining crew safely into Barmouth. The crew were from the French vessel *Medoc*, 604 tons, registered in Bordeaux and carrying a cargo of sugar from Havana to Liverpool. Captain Roux reported that *Medoc* had grounded on the causeway at about 2am that morning and had been taking in water. Subsequently, *Medoc* broke free from the causeway and with a north westerly behind her was drifting southwards. She was soon spotted from Aberystwyth, prompting the launch of the lifeboat *Evelyn Wood*. The scene that presented itself to the crew of the lifeboat can only be guessed at, but evidently deserted, her timbers creaking, decks awash and sails torn, *Medoc* must have looked quite eerie. Finding her deserted and sinking *Evelyn Wood* headed back to Aberystwyth. Exactly how long she stayed afloat is uncertain but on December 16th the following advertisement appeared in The Times: *"Notice to Mariners. West Coast – Cardigan Bay. Wreck off Aberystwyth. Trinity House, London Dec 14th 1869. Notice is hereby given that a green buoy marked "wreck" has been laid 20 fathoms NW of the wreck of the French vessel Medoc sunk off Aberystwyth. The buoy lies in 6 _ fathoms at low water spring tides with the following marks and compass bearings viz Aberystwyth SSE; Borth E by SE, Bwch head NNE by 1/2E"*

This puts the final resting place of the *Medoc* in the region of six miles off Borth.

Humility

Date wrecked 11th November 1872
Official no. 21502
Built Sunderland, 1828
Type of vessel Brig, 150 tons
Port of registry Weymouth

BORTH – Foundering of a ship off Borth – great excitement was caused among the inhabitants of Borth on Sunday Nov 10th by the appearance of a brig, Humility, of Weymouth bound from Poole to Runcorn with clay, which anchored near the shore. However as she showed no signs of distress she was not boarded. She continued to float all right until Monday afternoon when she went down and is likely to become

a total wreck. From the statement made by Wm Washer, the master, it seems that the brig is an old one, built in 1825. She became leaky on Oct 20th and had to put in at Plymouth. On the 9th inst the master found the vessel was making water from straining and although the pumps were kept going the vessel became unmanageable. On Sunday afternoon he tried to run to Aberdovey harbour, but failed and getting to leeward the vessel rode at anchor in five fathoms. At low water the vessel struck, the anchor having dragged. She is not insured. Some complaints have reached us because the Aberystwyth lifeboat did not go to the assistance of the vessel but from enquiries we have made it seems that their efforts, if required, would not have been successful, as there was an ebb tide and a strong wind against them.
Cambrian News 15/11/1872
The vessel's register was closed on 16th December 1872.

Moringen
Date wrecked 16th June 1877
Built Trondheim, 1862
Type of vessel Brig, 217 tons
Port of registry Drammen
Setting off from her home port on 26th May 1862 with a cargo of 250 tons of wood, mainly in the form of deals and battens, *Moringen* had an uneventful voyage until arriving off the coast of Wales on 15th June. She was noted as being sound with two working pumps, two boats and a crew of six. The next day - by the time the tide was judged suitable for crossing the Dyfi bar - a strong north-westerly wind was blowing and a heavy sea was running. It was by now one hour after high tide. Setting off across the bar in a south-easterly direction, the master had not anticipated the strength of the tide running against the vessel. Pushed to the south of the channel she soon bumped the sandy bottom, the impact carrying away her rudder. Captain Bergstrom and his crew were now aware that their vessel was in dire straits. By now hitting the sea-bed violently the crew attempted to ease the stress on the hull by cutting away the backstays and throwing the resultant debris overboard, the second mate nearly going with it. *Moringen* was now listing heavily to starboard and the crew only too aware of their predicament. The crew scrambled up the sloping deck to the port side aware that their lives were now in danger. Shortly after the deck cargo broke free and was washed away. The keel was carried away soon afterwards, followed closely by the sternpost. It was at this point that the Aberdyfi lifeboat came alongside and took the six exhausted and frightened sailors on board. *Moringen* became a total wreck.
The vessel was valued at £400, but insured for only £200, representing a considerable loss to her owners.
In 1970 the National Hydrographic Office reported traces of beams in the sand at 52 31 36N 004 02 27W. It is quite possible that these remains are those of the *Moringen*.

Western Seas

Date wrecked 12th January 1981
Official no. 337408
Built Seaton, Devon 1971
Type of vessel Motor boat
Port of Registry Aberystwyth

Owned jointly by local fisherman Keith Stone and local businessman Tony Meyler, *Western Seas* was a familiar site off the coast of Ceredigion. On this occasion she had been successfully trawling for sprats on the sandy terrain a mile or so off Borth. In the early hours of the 12th of January Keith Stone felt the engine slackening. Suspecting that the nets had become entwined round the propeller, he slipped the gear into neutral to try and free the fishing net from the propeller. This tactic didn't work. *Western Seas* was now in danger of drifting down on to her own nets and further compounding the problem. The anchor was set but, due to the nature of the seabed, the anchor failed to grip and the vessel continued to drift. Mayday signals were sent but, due to their inshore position the signals were hindered by the nearby hills and could not be picked up by the coastguard. Fortunately, the plight of *Western Seas* and her crew of two were observed from the shore and the coastguard roused. By now the engine room was starting to fill with water and the waves breaking against the vessel had stove in a number of windows in the wheelhouse. It was at this point that Keith Stone and Martin Leyland decided to abandon *Western Seas.* Grabbing the five available lifebelts and hastily tying them together they plunged into the breakers and struck for shore. After twenty minutes' struggle through the breakers the two men staggered safely ashore at Borth. Although *Western Seas* was later hauled up onto the beach at Borth the damage was too great for her to be repaired.

CHAPTER 6

Miscellany

As with many books on local history, there are always nuggets of information peripheral to the main body of the work. As they are at least as interesting as other tales related elsewhere in the book, it is the author's assertion that these also deserve to be recorded. There are also incidents that, due to their circumstances, will always retain a large element of mystery. Here are some such examples.

Howard

Date wrecked 2nd September 1891
Official number 82977
Built Neyland, 1884
Type of vessel Ketch, 50 tons
Port of registry Milford Haven

For the retired sailors and fishermen who congregated on the promenade near the bandstand September 2nd 1891 was not a promising day. Although bright and sunny, there was a brisk westerly wind, which had whipped up a heavy sea and put an end to their hopes of making a few shillings rowing tourists around the bay. Using a spyglass, John Humphreys and George White, both experienced seamen and members of the Royal Naval Reserve, picked out a vessel on the horizon to the north west. Moving slowly in a south-easterly direction, it became apparent that all was not well with the vessel, in fact she appeared positively distressed and was heading for Patches. They could see that she made little progress, and as she got closer the mainsail was seen flapping, the mizzen boom was dragging in the water and no one was hauling it in. Gathering some of their fellows around them they debated what course of action to take. The conditions were too rough to venture out of the harbour. Even had they been able to launch a sailing boat of some kind they estimated it would take until dawn to reach the vessel. The only option was *Gwladys*, a six-oared gig then on the main beach. Six oarsmen and a cox got into *Gwladys* in an attempt to reach the stricken vessel. Once they got away from the shelter of Castle Rocks conditions deteriorated, the sea became choppy and the boat started to take in water. The cox, as well as steering into the waves to prevent the boat broaching, was also engaged in bailing the boat. After two hours rowing and constant bailing the crew caught up with the stricken vessel. By now the vessel was about two miles off Llanrhystud and being blown broadside on towards the beach. Rolling heavily in the water she was difficult to board, but eventually this was achieved. Scrambling aboard, her new crew ascertained that the vessel was the *Howard* from Milford. Parts of her bulwarks were stove in, she was deserted, there was three feet of water in her hold and she was carrying a cargo of granite blocks. As her mizzen-mast was out of action, sails were set on the mainmast and with difficulty the vessel answered to the wheel and gradually came round.

Word had spread around the town as to the presence of a distressed ship out at sea so by the time *Howard* was brought into Aberystwyth harbour at 8pm crowds had gathered to view the spectacle. *Howard* was handed over to Mr Stephenson, Receiver of Wrecks, by the gallant salvors. By now there was much speculation as to the fate of the original crew. As the ship's anchor was stowed aboard, she had evidently not broken free from her moorings. Likewise, the ship's boat was still aboard and had not been used to effect an escape. It was surmised that the crew had been washed overboard. Subsequent enquiries revealed that the crew of three had been safely landed at Liverpool. *Howard* had set off from Falmouth some days previously but had encountered increasingly unsettled weather and heavy seas. When seventeen miles south east of Bardsey Island the cargo had shifted, and the vessel started to list. Seeing a steamer nearby, the crew signalled their distress and were taken aboard, later landing safely at Liverpool.

The vessel itself being fairly new was valued at £350, the cargo a further £202. Neither was insured. Following a meeting between the vessels master, owner, the aforementioned Receiver of Wrecks (Mr Stephenson) and the salvors each of the seven men who had ventured out to the Howard received fifteen pounds for their services, as did the owner of *Gwladys*. Fifteen pounds might not seem much by today's standards, but at this time a month's wages for an able-bodied seaman was three pounds ten shillings (£3.50p) a month.

SS Memphian

Date wrecked 8th October 1917
Official number 127902
Built 1908
Type of vessel Steamship, 6305 tons
Port of registry Liverpool

Although SS *Memphian* was sunk 7 miles ENE of the Arklow Light Vessel on the other side of the Irish Sea, her demise led to a tragedy at Borth that cost three local lives and, consequently, the author feels justified in including it in the book. *Memphian*, owned by F Leyland & Co, had already claimed her place in posterity. As the *Titanic* headed towards its fate SS *Memphian* was one of the vessels that warned her captain of icebergs in the vicinity.

Sailing from Liverpool in ballast and bound for New Orleans *Memphian* came into the sites of a German U-boat, probably U101. Without warning a torpedo ripped into the side of *Memphian* killing 32 of her crew.

Eleven days later wreckage from the *Memphian* started to be washed up on the shores of Ceredigion. A ships boat,

two lanterns and other wreckage marked *Memphian* appeared near New Quay. At Wallog – 8 hatches, 3 oars, 1 marked *Memphian* were recovered.
On Borth beach two bodies, two oars and a boathook appeared. Recovery of flotsam and jetsam could prove profitable, the finder being entitled to any proceeds received from their subsequent sale by HM Customs. At Borth on the 22nd of November, Mr James Davies of Wesleyan Place, Borth, went out in his rowing boat to go fishing and to see if any further wreckage from *Memphian* was in the bay. He took with him his nephew and another teenage boy. The conditions throughout were calm. As there were no witnesses to what happened, the incident that led to their deaths can only be guessed at. It seems that one of the three must have fallen in, the others in attempting to rescue him either fell in or tipped the boat. Despite the Aberystwyth lifeboat searching for nearly twelve hours, no trace was found of the men until the morning when their boat washed up on Aberdyfi bar. The incident is recorded on the war memorial at Borth.

Petunia

Date wrecked 25th -27th February 1923
Official no. 108437
Built Aberdeen, 1898
Type of vessel Steam trawler, 180 grt
Port of Registry Milford Haven

This aging trawler with a crew of nine left Milford Haven on 23rd February 1923 for the Cardigan Bay fishing grounds. This was usually a round trip of seven to twelve days for a trawler the size of *Petunia.* Two days later a fierce gale blew lasting for three days. The following week every returning trawler caught at sea in the gale came back to Milford Haven with varying degrees of damage. No concern was yet felt for the *Petunia,* even though a lifebuoy marked M23, the registration number of *Petunia,* was washed up on the beach at Wallog. It was a known fact that movable objects were frequently washed overboard from vessels during heavy weather. As the days passed into weeks and no sightings of *Petunia* were reported anxiety began to mount. The master of *Petunia,* Captain Leduer, was in the habit of calling from Fishguard on his way back to Milford, but no such call came. Exactly what happened, when or where will probably be never known. A month after the gale two other Milford trawlers, *Carrysfort* and *Penrice Castle,* were both well overdue and eventually listed as 'Lost all hands' taking the death toll to twenty one, leaving behind a total of sixty one dependents to be cared for. At a public meeting a fund was set up to raise £10,000 to be distributed to the widows and children of the fishermen. To this day, the single lifebuoy washed up at Wallog remains the only clue to the fate of *Petunia.*

Aberdeen

Date wrecked 11th March 1941
*Official no.*106676
Built Glasgow, 1896
Type of vessel Steam trawler, 68 tons
Port of Registry Lowestoft
Being a lowly trawler was no reason to be immune to the aggression of Hitler's Germany in 1941. *Aberdeen* set out from Milford Haven and was nearing the Cardigan Bay fishing grounds when she was spotted from the air, probably given away by the plume of smoke belching from her aging boilers. A lone bomber attacked dropping a heavy bomb just off her stern. Although not a direct hit, the bomb had done enough damage to the stern for *Aberdeen* to start taking in water. The captain ordered the crew of nine to take to the ships boat. Shortly after abandoning the sinking trawler a gale sprang up and by the time it had abated only two of the crew, both Belgian refugees, were still alive. Two days after the sinking of the *Aberdeen* the Dutch steamer *Perseus* was to suffer a similar fate further out into the Irish Sea.

Suandra

Date wrecked 23rd June 1976
Official no. 362635
Built Belgium
Type of vessel smack, 35grt
Port of Registry Fleetwood
Although looking to all intents and purposes the epitome of a shipwreck, the remains of *Suandra* in the mud at Cardigan were the result of abandonment rather than a true shipwreck. However the story is of sufficient interest to make it worthy of inclusion.
Suandra was regarded as an attractive and well-built vessel when she was brought to Cardigan. Of indeterminate age, she was originally built as a crabber but was used for a variety of purposes around Cardigan. The summer of 1976 is remembered (by those old enough) as a particularly hot summer. For the crew of *Suandra*, four miles off Cardigan Island, it got a little too hot on June 23rd when she caught fire. Their discomfort was compounded by the explosion of gas cylinders down in the hold. Her distress rockets were launched and observed at the RAE station at Aberporth. Fortunately their resident

tug, *Dolwen*, was on hand to come to the rescue. *Dolwen* was a powerful 116-ton vessel used to manoeuvre targets into place and was equipped with a strong water jet. This was used to extinguish the fire aboard *Suandra*. She was then towed to New Quay for the damage to be assessed. The deliberate destruction of vessels was commonplace in Cardiganshire in the nineteenth century but up to this point was thought to be a thing of the past. At dawn the following Saturday wisps of smoke were to be seen coming out of *Suandra*, as was something else. An early riser enjoying the summer morning saw a shadowy figure leaving Suandra in great haste. This time it seemed that skulduggery of some sort was in the air! *Suandra* was again rescued, this time the local fire brigade extinguishing the flames.

By now lacking a wheelhouse and a few other accoutrements regarded as desirable in a sea-going boat, she was towed up the Teifi river to Cardigan. Repair, it seems, was not viable and she has lain in the mud for the last thirty years. It is a tribute to her builders and the stout oak from which she was built that even now she is recognisable as a once fine vessel.

Suandra settling into the Teifi mud, her timbers finally starting to decay after 30 years of neglect.

INDEX

Dates in parentheses refer to the date a vessel was lost